METHOD IN MADNESS

METHOD IN MADNESS

Geopolitics in a changing world
Analysis and predictions

FREDERICK LAURITZEN

Kallipolis Publishing

Venice
2023

Cover Image: Caspar David Friedrich, Two Men
Contemplating the Moon, ca. 1825–30, Metropolitan
Museum of Art, New York

καινὰ λύων τὰ παλαιὰ νοούμενα τέτλαθι μέλλον

Dedicated

to

Delphine and Alexander

TABLE OF CONTENTS

i

PREFACE

The articles presented in this volume were published between April 2022 and October 2023 on the site of Kallipolis.co.uk, a political and cultural consultancy, established by Avedis Hadjian and me in 2022.

The aim of the articles, now chapters, is to point out the relevant historical background which has shaped and informed current events. They are not aimed at seizing the moment, but rather explaining some long-term narratives which are defining choices made by the protagonists of today's political affairs.

In every one of the texts, collected here, one may see the advice of Avedis, whom I thank, and the support of my wife and son.

Venice, November 2023

INTRODUCTION

Though this be madness, yet there is method in 't
Hamlet, Act 2 scene 2, Shakespeare

There is method (history) in madness (geopolitics). We stand back confused looking at the state of the world when we forget the historic and cultural reasons for decisions taken by the principal political actors.

Each time an action is taken, one must think if it is in reaction to another's behaviour and to whose advantage it is. We can no longer think in terms of Aristotle's weakness of will: the notion that a person or a country may take the wrong decision when it has a series of choices. Each person takes the best decision according to his/her criteria in defence of him/herself and for his or her own advantage:

the Socratic Paradox. It implies that mistaken decisions are simply mistakes and misreading of a situation. Not all political action is perfect. Studying the past allows one to develop a list of precedents which make it easier to disentangle the present. The more one knows about another country's past actions, the more one may distinguish between its willed actions and its mistakes. One can only really understand one's own people and another's country if one is comfortable and accepting of the sort of mistakes and instinctive answers we give, or others give during a crisis.

Polonius in Shakespear's Hamlet points out that the young prince is mad (simply because he is different than him) but that this madness may be understood as method, when one has the patience to see the motivation and precedent for Hamlet's behaviour from a different point of view.

We learn by induction. The more experience one has in a certain area of life, the more one has the instruments and data to inform our future actions. Today's geopolitics needs a sound footing in history to obtain a reasonable analysis which may provide solutions to our current problems.

There is method in today's madness.

1
THE MYTH OF THE WEST AND RUSSIA

22ⁿᵈ April 2022

The embassy in Tehran was besieged by the local population, was overrun, and the ambassador killed in 1829. He was Alexander Griboyedov (1795-1829), one of the chief Russian writers whose analysis of the relation between East and West in his play, Woe from Wit (1823), is still central and a key to the Russian view. The main character looks bewildered as a Frenchman from Bordeaux is lionized by Russian society and elevated to a pedestal, which he somehow does not deserve. The same observer famously claimed that Russia should imitate the Chinese, who in their complete isolation from the outside world, had preserved their integrity.

"If we could only take something from the Chinese: their contempt for the intellect of foreigners. When will we rise

above the fashion of imitating foreigners?" (act 3 scene 22).

Every Russian school child has read these lines: they are central to their culture. The tension between idealizing the West and rejecting it. This idolized West is the one which only they understand. Catherine the Great (1762-1796) bought the libraries of Diderot, Voltaire and the old master paintings of Sir Robert Walpole which are now in St. Petersburg, neglected and sold by the West. The Russian feels alone in preserving this culture which is now no longer central either to France or the UK. The past shapes the future for the Russian while we are living in an eternal present without past or future. Western diplomats must grin and bear long historical lectures from Russians, whose relevance escapes them.

The West and Russia are speaking different languages. Their aims are possibly the same, but their means of expression are so different, that incomprehension is the key feature. It is the deaf who will not listen. Each side is blind to the other's priorities. Griboyedov paid with his life for his ability to step back from his own society as well as defending its interests in writing the treatise of Turkmenchay, which defined the relations between Persia and Russia in 1828. He was almost a revolutionary, and his friends were arrested as Decembrists in 1825, but his

2

focus was solitary: distant yet engaged. The West and China, no longer offer a model of culture or isolation, as in the day of Griboyedov.

That is the question for Russians today: who are our friends? who do we admire? Such questions are the ones each country should ask itself before providing clear-cut judgements. Diplomacy is the art of communication, but if no one is listening, and no one is speaking, war should not be the answer.

2

Mariupol: gateway to Europe

Mariupol is now (in)famous for its destruction. Few of us had heard of it before the 24ᵗʰ of February 2022. We should have. The cultural question at the heart of the city is the very identity of Europe. There is a Greek speaking community in the city and area, which some quickly dismiss as being people brought by Catherine the Great (1762-1796) to settle the new city in 1778 (one of the Potemkin villages). They had fled from Turkish controlled Crimea. These people to this day speak a dialect which is not like standard modern Greek and scholars disagree if it a descendant of what was spoken in northern Greece, or from the area of North-Eastern Turkey, the Pontos.

The Pontic dialect has many features derived from the ancient Greek spoken in the ionic colonies of the 6th – 5th century BC. (for example, kepin = kipion showing no itacism, arguably characteristic of Byzantine Greek). If we say the Azov Greeks speak a language like the one spoken in Greece, we think they came from there. If we say they speak a Pontic dialect, we dismiss the link with continental Greece. It would mean that they were there before either the Turks or the Tatars arrived in the northern Black Sea. By the way 'Crimea' is the Tatar name for ancient Greek Tauris. It from the latter that the palace of Potemkin takes its name in Saint Petersburg: the Taurid Palace begun in 1783, when Mariupol was founded. In 1787, Goethe wrote his Iphigeneia in Tauris, precisely about Crimea. With this background in mind, the Russian Duma has recently proposed to change the name of Crimea to Tavrida.

During soviet times a Cyrillic alphabet was devised for Mariupol Greek, and translations were made from Russian and Ukrainian literary works (The lay of Igor and the Kozbar of Taras Shevchenko). It would indicate that the dialect was one of the languages of the Soviet Union, regardless of the origin.

Mariupol gives us three ways in which to look at Europe today: 1) connect it to a known present (Mariupol is a Modern Greek dialect) 2) connect to a distant past (Mariupol is historic remnant of displaced (?) Ancient/Byzantine communities 3) it is independent, and the past is irrelevant to the present. (Mariupol Greek is a minority language). These three options are the ones which define the outlook for the future of Ukraine: 1) a western nation; 2) a historically western nation; 3) an eastern nation.

Mariupol Greek may be one of the oldest dialects of a European language since some say its presence on the Black Sea is 2500 years old. However, the city of Mariupol should not be relegated to academic footnotes but teach us that destroying such a city and heritage means amputating a limb of the European body.

3

A Lutheran curia?

6ᵗʰ May 2022

The reform of the Curia has always been a top priority for the Catholic Church. Pope Francis has now enacted an extraordinary reform which will revolutionize the Catholic Church in manner reminiscent of the reforms enacted in France by king Louis XIV (1643-1715). The Apostolic Constitution, *Praedicate Evangelium*, will come into force on the 5ᵗʰ of May 2022. At that moment, each department of church government will no longer be headed necessarily by an ordained man, but it may be headed by a lay man or lay woman. This may be welcome news for many, but it removes an important geographic element and replaces it with lobby pressure groups.

The first open and official gathering of the Christians at the Council of Nicaea (325) in the Roman Empire was clear that each city could have one bishop. It meant that each bishop has always had a geographic constituency. In the Catholic church, even cardinals had a link with a diocese or a geographic area, and therefore each leader in the curia as well. If a layperson heads a ministry, there is no accountability at the level of the congregations, but only from superiors in Rome. Louis XIV improved the efficiency of the ruling class of France, by diminishing the role of the aristocracy, which had allegiance to geographic constituencies (their lands), bringing them to Versailles and putting the power into the hands of bureaucrats. Within two generations the bureaucratic class had got rid of the monarchy and the aristocracy with the French Revolution (1789). The idea pursued by Pope Francis is that being ordained should no longer give a privileged path to power. Each catholic faithful is equal before the eyes of God. That was exactly what Martin Luther (1483-1546) argued when he proposed that each believer is like a priest without being ordained.

It is pure invention that pope, bishops, priests and monks are to be called the "spiritual estate"; princes, lords, artisans, and farmers the "temporal estate." (Martin Luther, *Letter to the Christian Nobility*, 1520).

Francis is the first Pope to have quoted Luther in the Sistine chapel. He prayed with Lutherans in Lund, Sweden on the 31st of October 2016. The Vatican issued a Stamp to commemorate the 500th anniversary of the Protestant Reformation and which depicted Luther and Melanchthon.

Moreover, the importance of the Laity is also central to the Orthodox world, where monks are technically laymen (and not ordained priests). If the laity becomes a class of bureaucrats, what is the potential career path for an ordained priest? It may be a better choice not to become a member of the priesthood. The (in)famous Talleyrand was ordained in 1780 and became bishop of Autun in 1788. With the revolution he left the priesthood, married, and pursued a successful political and diplomatic career.

Will the ordained be tempted to become laypersons to pursue their ambitions?

4

PROMETHEUS UNCHAINED
ELECTIONS IN SOUTH OSSETIA

13ᵗʰ May 2022

S itting comfortably in an armchair in front of a roaring fire in gloomy weather and reading about the recent Ossetian elections and the victory of Alan Glagoyev (Nykhaz party) on the 10ᵗʰ May 2022, own's mind would be forgiven if it wandered in the realm of comparative mythology and Indo-European linguistics. Indeed, the name of George Dumézil (1898-1986) could emerge together with his notion of an original European tripartite society made of king, priest, and soldier. The French scholar invented structuralist analysis by comparing Greek, Scandinavian and Ossetian mythology.

However, for the local inhabitants, things are cruder and more concrete. Anatoly Bibilov (United Ossetia party), has lost his re-election bid, as president of the Republic of

South Ossetia, a state not recognized by any other country. One of the reasons, is Ukraine. He sent his army to fight in the 'special operation' and some soldiers have come back complaining that the Russian army is in disastrous shape, as leaked on an opposition media outlet Mediazona (3rd May 2022). Bibilov campaigned for annexation to Russia, in case of success at the polls. This reveals a deep-seated problem in Russian politics. The Ossetian language is made of two main dialects: Iron and Digor. They are spoken only in north Ossetia whose capital is Vladikavkaz, a Potemkin village founded in 1784 and is part of the Russian Federation. Only Iron is spoken in South Ossetia a breakaway part of Georgia, under an alleged independence since 1991. Before that date it formed an Autonomous Oblast within the Soviet Union. They are two distinct cultures and two different languages. Superficially they are similar and here lies the problem.

Alexander Solzhenitsyn (1918-2008) also pointed out his shock when he discovered the animosity felt by the Ukrainians against Russia, which he described in the Archipelago Gulag (Book 5 chapter 2). He clearly did not expect that a brotherly Slavic culture could be so hostile. Hostility is sometimes the result of claims to the same area, language, or culture. Distance creates laziness and numbness. The special operation, or war, in Ukraine is precisely such a claim by two parties to the same culture and area. However, South Ossetia is not distant, they speak an Indo-European language, the only Iranian people not to convert to Islam. The nearest and tallest mountain maybe where Prometheus was chained (Kazbeg) and thus famous from Greek mythology and even tragedy (Aeschylus).

The new president will be sworn in on the 24th of May 2022. He studied at the University of Tskhinvali in South Ossetia. The university is notable for its partnerships with the Universities of Lugansk and Donetsk in the Donbass region. Ossetia reveals the continued issue of ethnic groups and nationalities which had been the subject of Stalin's book 'Marxism and the national question' of 1913. Putin advocated a multi-ethnic state in his 9th of May speech in Red Square this year, the same claim made by Milošević in his 'Gazimestan' speech in Kosovo on the 28th of June 1989. Both statements originate from bureaucratic language typical of communist states.

Times have changed. Yugoslavia taught us, by its demise, that attention must be sharp when discussing ethnic minorities. Indeed, Stalin divided North and South Ossetia in 1924, fearing the flaring of ethnic tensions within Georgia or Russia. Internal dynamics can evolve and escape the notice of the so called 'great powers' which then watch powerlessly as new situations unfold, incapable of reading new data, with new eyes. The election in South Ossetia has revealed local dynamics which are different from North Ossetia and the Russian Federation. South Ossetia may be a thermometer of a wider situation and sentiment and brings to the fore the issue of minorities and nations within Russia.

While thinking of these distant lands in the armchair, we may be listening to classical music, such as conducted by the most famous Osset, Valery Gergiev, conductor of the Mariinsky Theatre orchestra of Saint Petersburg. He not only conducted a victory concert in Palmyra in Syria on the 5th of May 2014, but more relevantly he led his orchestra in playing the Leningrad Symphony in Tskhinvali on the 21st of August 2008 after the short Ossetian-Georgian war. Let's not let the music wash over us with numb and comfortable disinterest, the Caucasus may yet teach us more about areas closer to our current attention.

5

SOLZHENITSYN ON UKRAINE 1968

20ᵗʰ May 2022

Alexander Solzhenitsyn (1918-2008) opened long ago the pandora's box of Ukraine. Fifty-five years ago, he explained the hostile attitude of Ukrainians towards Russia he encountered in Soviet prison camps. Instead of analysis this text needs to be quoted:

Written in 1968, published in 1974. (The Gulag Archipelago, Part 5, Chapter 2):

... It pains me to write this as Ukraine and Russia are merged in my blood, in my heart, and in my thoughts. But extensive experience of friendly contacts with Ukrainians in the camps has shown me how much of a painful grudge they hold. Our generation will not escape from paying for the mistakes of our fathers.

To stamp one's foot and shout: "This is mine!" is the easiest option. It is far more difficult to say: "Those who want to live, live!" Surprising as it may be, the Marxist doctrine that nationalism is fading has not come true.

On the contrary, in an age of nuclear research and cybernetics, it has for some reason flourished. And the time is coming for us, whether we like it or not, to repay all the promissory notes of self-determination and independence, to do it ourselves rather than wait to be burnt at the stake, drowned in a river or beheaded.

Revealing the dark side of the soul after 17 years in the Gulag

We must prove whether we are a great nation not with the vastness of our territory or the number of peoples in our care but with the greatness of our deeds. And with the degree to which we plough what we shall have left after those lands that will not want to stay with us secede.
With Ukraine, things will get extremely painful. But one must understand the degree of tension they feel. As it has been impossible for centuries to resolve it, it is now down to us to show good sense.

We must hand over the decision-making to them: federalists or separatists, whichever of them wins. Not to give in would be mad and cruel. The more lenient, patient, coherent we now are, the more hope there will be to restore unity in the future.

Let them live it, let them test it. They will soon understand that not all problems are resolved through separation. Since in different regions of Ukraine there is a different proportion of those who consider themselves Ukrainians, those who consider themselves Russians and those who consider themselves neither, there will be many difficulties there.

Maybe it will be necessary to have a referendum in each region and then ensure preferential and delicate treatment of those who would want to leave. Not the whole of Ukraine in its current formal Soviet borders is indeed Ukraine.

Some regions on the left bank [of the river Dnepr] clearly lean more towards Russia. As for Crimea, Khrushchev's decision to hand it over to Ukraine was arbitrary. And what about Carpathian (Red) Ruthenia? That will serve as a test too: While demanding justice for themselves, how just will the Ukrainians be to Carpathian Russians?

April 1981. From a letter to the Toronto conference on Russo-Ukrainian relations, Harvard Ukrainian Research Institute. Published in Russkaya Mysl, June 18, 1981. In

Russia, published for the first time in the magazine Zvezda, No 12, 1993.

6
SWEDISH NEUTRALITY
BETWEEN THE COSSACKS AND UKRAINE

3ʳᵈ June 2022

Sweden is politically neutral yet culturally western. The Russian invasion of Ukraine has changed this balance. Carl Bildt, foreign Minister of Sweden (2006-2014), had already expressed reservations about the annexation of Crimea in 2014 in some tweets and more recently as well. Putin had claimed that the fact that Crimea was part of Ukraine was a mistake of historic analysis. Since it had been part of Russia in the past, it should allegedly be part of Russia again today. Bildt indicated that it was Valdemar who had been baptised, not Vladimir, or Volodymyr, i.e. that the first Christian king of Rus was actually a viking from Sweden and therefore his country could make an equal claim to Crimea. Indeed, Sweden is not indifferent to the question of Ukraine, since the descendant of Valdemar/Vladimir/Volodimyr was Yaroslav of Kiev (1019-1054) whose symbol, a trident, appeared on his coins and is now the national symbol of

Ukraine. Carl Bildt thus claimed that the Viking Rurikid dynasty of Rus would give Sweden today historic claims to that part of the world. Sweden is careful and aware of its history and role in the Baltic and the wider world.

It is for this reason that Sweden has been neutral since 1815. The Congress of Vienna (1814-1815) had decided this fate for the kingdom. Sweden had changed sides in the Napoleonic wars and the French general Jean Bernadotte, became Charles XIV (1818-1844) the Swedish king. The turning point was the largest battle ever fought before World War I, the battle of Leipzig 16th – 19th October 1813, in which Charles Stewart, brother to the British foreign secretary, Viscount Castlereagh (1812-1822), convinced Bernadotte to join the Austrian, Prussian and Russian forces and gave Marshal Blücher his most important and famous victory, before his decisive intervention at Waterloo in 1815. The premise of Swedish neutrality is therefore the essential location of the country in relation to the Baltic Sea. The neutrality continued also during World War II and during the cold war the Sweden navy observed NATO and Soviet submarines enter its territorial waters and discharge depth charges to make them leave.

Sweden has now abandoned the neutral status for fear that the expansionist policy of the Russian Federation would affect the Baltic as well as its neighboring countries changing a centuries old status quo. Sweden bordered with the Russian empire between 1805 and 1917, when to the east it had the Grand Duchy of Finland. Sweden has only been superficially neutral since the Russians invaded by crossing the frozen Gulf of Bothnia in 1808 and since a Swedish archipelago, the Åland islands, was also invaded by Russia in 1809 and annexed to Finland (to this day). This last invasion was carried out by Cossacks, from the area of Ukraine, under the Baltic German general Gotthard Johann von Knorring (1746-1825). Indeed, these islands were later the location for a battle of the Crimean War and were once more defended by Cossacks. Sweden remembers its encounters with Russians and Cossacks at home and so has abandoned the neutrality imposed on it in 1815.

7

SEISMIC CHANGE IN MOSCOW PATRIARCHATE

9ᵗʰ June 2022

The Russian Orthodox church depends on stability in the Kremlin and therefore is an accurate thermometer about the situation in Ukraine as seen from Moscow. Not only had Moscow changed the church's jurisdiction in Crimea, Hilarion Alfeyev, Metropolitan of Volokolamsk, and head of the Foreign Affairs of the Moscow Patriarchate has been removed from this position on the 7ᵗʰ of June 2022 and sent to Hungary as new Metropolitan of Budapest. Thus, Viktor Orban, the president of Hungary, has effectively placed himself at the centre of future negotiations between the Catholic Church and the Russian Orthodox Church. Leaving Hungary aside, this decision is seismic. Alfeyev had held the top diplomatic office at the Moscow Patriarchate since 2009. In addition to his dismissal, on the 7ᵗʰ of June the synod of the patriarchate voted several significant decisions:

The establishment of the position of 'archpriest / protopresbyter' of the military and naval clergy which existed before 1918. The head of it will be Oleg Ovcharov (former Rector of Yaroslav Theological Seminary). Anthony of Korsun, a close collaborator of Patriarch Kirill, and well acquainted with Italy since he looked after Russian church buildings in Italy, is now head of Foreign Relations of the Moscow Patriarchate. The diocese of Crimea has become directly dependent on the Moscow Patriarchate. In 2011 Patriarch Kirill (when Hilarion was head of Foreign Affairs) refused to include the breakaway regions of Abkhazia and South Ossetia under the jurisdiction of Moscow and therefore retained the traditional canonical jurisdiction.

The change of Crimea is therefore significant. Combined with the creation of an archpriest for the naval forces, it seems that the Black Sea Fleet based in Crimea is requesting more attention. It is also significant that no other changes are made in Russian occupied Ukraine. The resolution, however, indicates that the Orthodox in Ukraine are not commemorating Kirill during the services. This means that canon 15 of the Synod of Constantinople of 861 plays a role, since it refers to the situation in which a priest does not commemorate a schismatic patriarch or bishop. In other words, not praying for Kirill means that there is a division *de facto*, but not yet *de iure*. Chaos.

Indeed, the Moscow Patriarchate has put a trusted person as head of foreign affairs. There are two possible reasons: Kirill no longer trusts Hilarion, who has condemned the war in Ukraine (in general terms) together with all other Orthodox churches at the World Council of Churches on the 17th of May 2022. He was removed shortly after that. Another option is that he will use Hilarion as resident in Budapest to establish a direct channel between the Vatican and Moscow via Budapest. That would explain why Orban refused to impose sanctions on Patriarch Kirill. Both may be true. Hilarion may be aiming to succeed Kirill as patriarch of Moscow after the new order is established at the end of the war in Ukraine. Kirill has lost support within the Russian Orthodox Church and may simply be powerless.

Such speculation is a matter of dreams. The synod document points to problems of jurisdiction, problems with the opinion within the armed forces in Crimea (especially the Black Sea Fleet), and, more fundamentally, it may indicate the permanent loss of Moscow Parishes in Ukraine. Moscow is calling for a reset of relations and help from this quagmire. Maybe the Kremlin feels the same. But isn't too late?

8

CLAUSEWITZ ON UKRAINE

Putin has said that he does not want Russia to suffer the fate of the Soviet Union, in the case of defeat. We are finally hearing that the 'special operation' is in fact a war. Each party in a war wishes to win. An honourable armistice, or end of hostilities is ideal, especially from a civilian point of view. The reality of war is about winning. Winning means defeating the other country. Defeat means the victor has the power to decide the fate of the other country. We are no longer used to thinking of war as something so overwhelming for the defeated country. We think of war as an economic battle in which each party is gaining substantial amounts of wealth through arms deals and reconstruction contracts. The head of the European Commission, Ursula von der Leyen has stated the EU's interest in reconstructing Ukraine.

We need to go back to von Clausewitz (1780-1831) and his treatise on War (1832): *"war is an act of violence intended to compel our opponent to fulfil our will"*. He then continues: *"Now, philanthropists may easily imagine there is a skilful method of disarming and overcoming an enemy without great bloodshed, and that this is the proper tendency of the Art of War. However plausible this may appear, still it is an error which must be extirpated; for in such dangerous things as War, the errors which proceed from a spirit of benevolence are the worst. As the use of physical power to the utmost extent by no means excludes the co-operation of the intelligence, it follows that he who uses force unsparingly, without reference to the bloodshed involved, must obtain a superiority if his adversary uses less vigour in its application. The former then dictates the law to the latter, and both proceed to extremities to which the only limitations are those imposed by the amount of counter-acting force on each side"*.

Putin is now reacting to such statements. If Russia is to lose in Ukraine, what will the consequences be for Russia? His statement indicates that he fears such a defeat may not only be achieved by Ukraine alone but ultimately combined with NATO. He has also talked about the partition of Russia, as the Soviet Union was also disintegrated in 1991 in the case of defeat.

Clausewitz indicates that there are three aims in war: 1) invasion and occupation 2) to aim for those strategic objectives which will do most harm to the enemy 3) wearing out the enemy.

One may add that if Russia is worn out, the internal national tensions of the Federation could emerge and risk a sort of implosion or even partition into zones of influence. The Far East to China, the West to the EU and neutral vis-a-vis NATO. However, the real risk is a permanent conflict in the Caucasus. The West may be worn out too, depleted economically and militarily. Russia and NATO could be exhausted, while Ukraine is crushed between them.

China would then emerge energized and a well-rested onlooker. China delayed the Russian operation until the end of the Olympics were over, at the time when the mud in Ukraine (rasputitsa) makes any invasion impossible. It stopped providing spare parts to Russian airplanes in March and decreed a no-fly zone for Russian planes in May. In the meantime, Europe is restless about the economic mayhem ahead and putting its head in the sand about Eastern Europe's concerns and fears.

Clausewitz was right, the defeated party is the one which is worn out. NATO, Russia, and Ukraine could soon be exhausted. At that point, the winner is China.

9

THE POPE'S CHOICE AND THE VERSAILLES DILEMMA

17ᵗʰ June 2022

Pope Francis has claimed that the Russian war in Ukraine has been provoked by forces external to Russia (14.6.22). The Vatican had already indicated that it considered Ukrainians and Russians in the same way. The *Via Crucis* Easter procession in Rome's Colosseum had two women, one from Ukraine, and one from Russia carrying a cross together (15.4.22). This symbolism was lost on Catholics from Eastern Europe. The Ukrainian Catholic church forbade the transmission of the event on Ukrainian TV. Catholics in Poland were outraged. The Ukrainian embassy in Rome presented a formal complaint to the Vatican.

The statement of the Pope coincides with the nomination of a new Russian Orthodox Metropolitan of Budapest, Hilarion Alfeyev, who had been head of foreign relations for the Moscow Patriarchate from 2009 to 2022. Hungary is a Catholic country. While we remember that Viktor Orban is the controversial president of Hungary, we sometimes forget that Eduard Habsburg Lothringen has been Hungarian Ambassador to the Vatican since 2015. His Habsburg cousin Archduke William of Austria fought in Ukraine during world war I and II and wrote poetry in Ukrainian and died in a Soviet prison in 1948. The Habsburg family has always had an interest in Catholicism as well as Ukraine. The Pope thus has strengthened a direct channel with Moscow: Patriarch Kirill can now speak to Pope Francis though Metropolitan Hilarion, President Orbán and the Habsburg ambassador to the Holy See.

This opens the door to the question of the treatise of Versailles of 1919. Most who looked at the treatise after 1919 found and pointed out flaws in the different provisions which put an end to world war I. In the same way the settlement of Ukraine signed by Boris Yeltsin, Bill Clinton, and Leonid Kravchuk on the 14th of January 1994 has often been considered flawed. The US promised no expansion of NATO and Russia promised not to invade Ukraine. Promises have been broken. In the same way provisions of Versailles were broken or altered.

However, the key moment concerning the treatise of Versailles of 1919 came on the 1st of September 1939. On that day German armed forces crossed the Polish border and began the invasion of Poland. From that day on, no one considered the flaws of Versailles any longer. The treatise was shelved within the footnotes of history ready to be studied by historians isolated from reality, but no longer relevant to politicians immersed in day-to-day administration. The Russian invasion of Ukraine on the 24th of February 2022 has wiped off the map all treatises concerning Ukraine. That may have been one of Russia's aims. Putin clearly indicated in his 9th of May 2022 speech on Red Square the need for a new congress system. He meant something like the Congress of Vienna (1815) or the Potsdam Conference (1945) in which Russia participated as a victor and drew new lines across Europe.

Russia aims to be at the negotiating table with the US, NATO and Ukraine. China will probably be the decisive, even if apparently silent, observer at such a meeting. Putin has brought Russia back on the negotiating table for Ukraine's future and removed the treatises agreed before the 'special operation'. Each inch of land conquered by Russia in Ukraine will be exchanged for favourable conditions and contracts (oil, gas, minerals) for the Russian Federation.

It appears that the channel opened by Pope Francis is focusing on the balance established in the 90s between Ukraine and Russia. The Vatican will not be at the negotiating table, but the delay in condemning Russia will contribute to ever more favourable negotiating conditions for the Russians.

Invading another country is a breach of international law and war is a breach of religious morality. The need for peace is imperative, but war should be condemned first by religious authorities on humanitarian grounds and without ambiguity.

10

UKRAINE CAUGHT BETWEEN ROMAN AND INTERNATIONAL LAW

24th June 2022

Russia has crossed the Ukrainian border with its army and now occupies circa 20% of Ukraine's territory. All countries recognize the borders of Ukraine as they stood before the 24th of February 2022. The de facto borders are different from the de iure ones.

Borders are a contribution of Roman legal thought to European civilization. Hadrian's Wall in Scotland is a visible Roman border. A border divided two different legal systems. Within Roman borders, since 212 AD everyone was a Roman citizen (edict of Caracalla) and had the right to an equal treatment before the law. Starting from 533AD, contradictory laws were eliminated, and the code of Roman law was issued in Constantinople (today's Istanbul), the capital of the Roman Empire. It applied to all those living within Roman borders. Those outside the Roman polity, lived with overlapping and contradictory legal codes, with uncertain definitions of crimes and punishments. Those who were not Roman citizens looked in admiration. The Arabs adopted the Byzantine word for customs house (*jumruk* in Arabic – *gümrük* in Turkish – from Greek *kommerkiarion*/κομμερκιάριον). Turkish adopted the East Roman word for border (Greek *synoron* / σύνορον – Turkish *sınırı*).

Borders and customs represented certainty. Clear terms guarantee valid commercial contracts and flourishing trade. They mean collaboration is possible even among those who are not familiar or even unacquainted with each other. Disrupting borders and custom houses means fudging the distinction between two types of law: national and international. The Romans distinguished between civil law (*ius civile*) and the law of nations (*ius gentium*). Civil law cases were regulated by courts and tribunals and concerned only Roman citizens. Law of nations was used for international relations and allowed the contact between different legal systems but were the exclusive competence of the Roman emperor who had only his instinct to decide such cases. Putin has decided to limit the territory where Ukrainian civil law applies. Yet he has not incorporated the conquered territories into the Russian civil jurisdiction.

The war zone is a situation of legal chaos. Civilian life cannot continue.

The collapse of Roman civil law ushered what some might call the Dark Ages. The demise of this secure legal system brought social instability which progressed towards political uncertainty. The value of Roman civil law today is that it reveals how weak international law is. Indeed, the Roman emperor provided an army to support his claims within international law when a conflict rose with another country. Today armies defend the internal constitution of countries. Putin has taken advantage of the defenceless nature of international relations and keeps advancing since no one knows how to stop him. The Russian Parliament will discuss a law proposal (presented by Fëodorov) to cancel the recognition of Lithuania as an independent country. The proposal claims that the recognition of the independence of Lithuania is allegedly worthless according to the internal laws of the Soviet Union, and its successor state, Russia. It is a legal point of view, and rather legalistic, that reveals that international law has no instruments to counter such an argument. If the duma adopts such a law, the west will send a letter to complain rather than take any action. Lithuania is worried, as are all other Baltic states and several Eastern European EU and NATO member states.

Putin advances into Ukraine and suspends civil law in the occupied areas, while cancelling international treaties with Russian national law. Such a legalistic approach does not accept the principles of Roman law, based on the distinction between *ius civile* and *ius gentium*, a defining element of European civilization.

11

UKRAINE AS A NEW SILESIA?
PUTIN AND FREDERICK THE GREAT

1ˢᵗ July 2022

Putin spent too much time in East Germany. What he learnt he has applied to Ukraine. The KGB posted him in Dresden between 1985-1990, apparently as a translator. Dresden was in an area devoid of West German television signals, and therefore was known as the 'Tal der Ahnunglosen,' the 'valley of the clueless. Dresden was also the main seat of the Russian army in East Germany (1945-1990). However, Dresden is a chief example of the military strategy of Frederick II of Prussia, 'Frederick the Great' (1740-1786). He avoided Dresden during his attack on Saxony in 1760 but brought great destruction to the city. He often went around cities rather than conquer them to make field advances. This was the case when he invaded Silesia on the 16ᵗʰ December 1740. By the 9ᵗʰ of January 1741 he had conquered Breslau (Wroclaw in Poland) and therefore the whole of Silesia was part of Prussia.

Putin imagined Ukraine as a modern Silesia. Frederick the Great thought he had a natural claim to Silesia because the region spoke the same language but was culturally part of Austria. When the ruler of Austria, Charles VI had died in October 1740, Frederick did not recognize his successor Maria Theresa of Austria. In the same way, after Angela Merkel, Olaf Scholz became the new chancellor on the 8th December 2021. Two months later, Putin attacked Ukraine.

Putin's invasion of Ukraine could lead to a worldwide conflict. Frederick the Great with his invasion of Silesia provoked not only the first Silesian war, but two others. The third one is known as the Seven Year war (1756-1763). In the US it is known as the French Indian war, focusing on a local theatre. The treaty of Paris which settled the war (1763) saw the largest ever acquisition of territory by any country by treaty: the United Kingdom gained Canada and India. Pitt the Elder, later prime minister of the UK (1766-1768) famously said: 'Canada will be won on the battlefields of Silesia'. Unlike Prussia then, Russia now appears to have no allies and to have started something which is out of its control.

Frederick's misjudgement about Dresden was noticed by Napoleon, who even owned a bust of the king of Prussia.

Napoleon attacked, besieged, and occupied Dresden in 1805 to prove Frederick had been wrong on this occasion. He respected Frederick the Great so much that he went to visit his tomb in 1806 and said: 'if he were alive today, we would not be here'. East Germany considered Frederick the Great as a great strategist and model for subsequent German armies. He was studied in the military academies of the East German Army and Putin, in his formative years in East Germany, lived in a world which considered Frederick as the military strategist par excellence. The respective merits of Frederick the Great and Napoleon were studied by Clausewitz, an officer of the Prussian Army, in his work 'On War' (1832).

Putin seems to have used Silesia as a model for Ukraine. He thought he was achieving goals like the First Silesian War (1740-1742). Putin forgot that Frederick won the war because of two miracles: internal conflicts with the enemy coalition in 1759 and the death of the empress of Russia of 1762, followed by an unexpected ceasefire. The NATO summit of Madrid makes any miracle to save Russia almost unimaginable. Countries like China and Iran are not military allies but seem to be taking over the Russian economy to the detriment of the Kremlin and the welfare of the population. Putin is not Frederick the Great and Ukraine is not Silesia. Let's hope this is not start of a worldwide war.

12
ALL ROADS LEAD TO KALININGRAD

8ᵗʰ July 2022

Kaliningrad is typically European. A forgotten economic wasteland with a great history. It is the only Baltic port of the Russian Federation which is not blocked by ice in the winter. It is enclosed by a lagoon on which the German writer Thomas Mann, famous for Death in Venice (1912), had his holidays. His summer house is now a museum in Neringa in Lithuania. Kaliningrad used to be known as Königsberg and was the capital of Prussia. In 1947 Prussia ceased to exist by treaty (US, UK, FR, URSS). All the population (predominantly German) abandoned the city. Half of Prussia is today part of the Russian Federation including Kaliningrad.

Prussia is now a mythical name, in good and bad, but few are interested in historic reality. The Prussians were originally a Slavic people who settled the area around this lagoon. They spoke a language extinct which did not survive the arrival of German speakers mainly in the 13th century. One forgets that the reason for the arrival of these settlers was the destruction brought by the Mongol expansion which stretched from Korea to Legnica (Leignitz) (on today's German Polish border) in 1241. The wasteland created by these invasions was subsequently filled by German settlers along the Baltic shores.

Prussia became a catholic monastic state administered by knights, the Teutonic knights, in 1224. This state existed until the head of the chivalrous order decided to abandon celibacy, get married, and become ruler of Prussia by becoming protestant in 1525 (Prussia was the first protestant state). He asked for help from his uncle, the king of Poland. Prussia was strongly connected with all countries with which it bordered. There were many contacts and contaminations within the Baltic area. Kaliningrad today is an isolated monument to a transplanted people: the modern inhabitants are Russian.

The annihilation of Prussia in 1947 was not combined with a solution for the area. Today we are yet again living a 'Prussian' problem. We do not look at the past and yet continuously live with it and suffer from our lack of curiosity of the origins of peoples, places, and countries.

Konigsberg (Kaliningrad) was important from 1224 to 1701. From then it lived a slow decline. Berlin became the centre of Prussian power, even though every ruler was crowned in Königsberg until 1701. The ruling family of Prussia, the Hohenzollern, promoted studies that indicated that the Goths, when they left modern day Sweden, settled in Prussia and then went on to attack the Roman Empire, defeating the western half and creating the first kingdom of Italy with capital in Ravenna in 476. Their king, Theoderic, created some of the famous mosaics there. It is for this reason that the Hohenzollerns brought some of them to Berlin and Potsdam where they are in display today. Prussia was a European region. Kaliningrad is historically a crossroads east-west but also north-south. It cannot survive on its own but needs unfettered interaction with neighbours. Kaliningrad needs open roads to and from it.

Creating an island of Russianness in 1947 was short-sighted. Kaliningrad can only thrive as part of the European Union. However, the EU prefers to recreate a scenario which will lead to war. Kaliningrad should not become a new Danzig (today Gdansk). The Free city of Danzig (also in Prussia) was the casus belli for Germany on 1st September 1939. The technical reason was the protection of the corridor connecting Germany and Danzig through Polish territory. In a short sighted move the EU is proposing a corridor for Kaliningrad (the Siwalki corridor).

13
PUTIN'S PLAN FOR THE PARTITION OF RUSSIA

15th July 2022

Russia fears partition. After the division of Poland in 1772, 1793, 1795 and Germany in 1945, it starts to suspect it might be next, due to the hatred the West allegedly nourishes towards Russia. The West is out to damage, destroy and divide the Russian Federation, possibly according to the principle of self-determination proposed by President Wilson in the discussions at the end of world war I. Russophobia is a Russian government keyword. Putin is claiming lands which were allegedly historically Russia but are outside its borders. He is disrespecting the notion of international borders. Accordingly, there is a project in the Duma to scrap the recognition of Lithuania, meaning it is still legally part of Russia.

Russophobia is a smoke screen. The liberal party (right wing) has proposed yet again that the Russian term 'president' is a foreign loan word and should be replaced by 'pravitel' something like 'legislator'. In fact, they are proposing the name of 'supreme leader of Russia' (Верховный правитель России). The title was used by the white Russians who fought against the Bolshevik revolution and established a counter-revolutionary government of southern Russia (1918-1920) a month after Nicholas II was executed.

This government represented the first partition of Russia. The cities of Petrograd (Leningrad) and Moscow were under the Bolsheviks and the South of Russia (essentially today's Ukraine) formed an alternative government. The White Russian State was dissolved in 1920 and somehow continued in the far East (Priamurie) until 1923. The revolutionary and counter revolutionary capitals, Moscow, on the one hand, and a succession of capitals for the White Russians, reveal how Russia risks being partitioned today: Ufa (1918); Omsk (1918-1920); Vladivostok (1921-1923), which served as capitals for the counter-revolutionary forces during the Civil War. The regions would centre round Urals, Siberia, the Far East. The Southern Russian Government had a seat in Sebastopol (Crimea).

No one should want such a partition, but Putin has put it on the drawing board because of the invasion of Ukraine.

Without the 'special operation', such a division would have been a far-flung fantasy. In a war one cannot only imagine a victorious scenario but also what one may lose in case of defeat. Putin has effectively offered the partition of Russia, if he loses this war.

The flashback to the early twentieth century points to a fundamental issue of today's Russia. The reforms begun by Nicholas II, were interrupted by the October revolution. Some of them are being discussed today, as if 1917-1991 never occurred. Putin claimed it was the fault of the soviets if different republics were established in former Russian territory. His collaboration with the Orthodox Church, and specifically with the Patriarch of Moscow is possible because of the reestablishment of the patriarchate in 1917 (it had been abolished by Peter the Great). The Orthodox sect of 'name worshiping' (*imaslavye* Имяславие) popular in the early twentieth century (and then condemned as a heresy) find support of the former head of foreign relations of the Moscow Patriarchate, Hilarion of Volokolamsk (2009-2022). The Duma itself was established in 1905 and abolished during Soviet times, to be recreated in 1993. The proposed land reforms of 1907-1911 still await implementation.

Behind the appearance of nostalgic references to the period 1905-1917 towers the figure whose reforms lead to remarkable economic growth and widespread social discontent: Pyotr Stolypin (interior minister 1906-1911). Stolypin was born in Dresden (where Putin was stationed) and was killed by a Ukrainian in Kiev. Members of the government who worked together with Stolypin were part of the different partitioned governments of Russia after the assassination of Nicholas II and fought against the Bolsheviks.

The language of pravitel / leader is intimately connected with reforms which brought wealth to some and social discontent to many at the end of the tsarist period. The term pravitel implies the partition of Russia. Putin is trapped in the language of Stolypin's reforms and their failed attempt to stop revolution. The titles adopted by the white Russian governments were established after Petrograd and Moscow were already centres of Soviet power. Using such titles and honours reminds Russians of exiled governments and short-lived political solutions. If Putin wants to assume the title of supreme leader, he is implicitly admitting defeat and offering his enemies at the peace table a plan to partition Russia.

14
MYKOLAIV AND ROMAN POETRY

27ᵗʰ July 2022

Putin aims to dominate nature. He has claimed that areas outside the recognized borders are part of the Russian Federation. He has a selective historic memory. Those countries were part of Russia in 1912, but not in 1712, and many were still independent states in 1812. Moreover, Slavic nations rose because of the settlement after a period of migration. The Greeks and Romans never encountered the Slavs. The natural obstacles found by these travelling peoples have not changed.

Famous is the description of Caesar's bridge built over the river Rhine (*De Bello Gallico*, Book 4). The bridge built in 54 BC employed a technique unknown to the local Germanic peoples who often identified easy crossing points with the word 'furt'. Many German or Austrian towns have that term today: Frankfurt, Erfurt, Klagenfurt. Even the town of Oxford indicates an easy crossing point with the term Saxon version of the word: 'ford'. The 'other place', Cambridge, also indicates a crossing with the term 'bridge'. These easy crossing points were crucial because migrants did not know how to cross rivers in the 'migration period', formerly known as the 'barbarian invasions'.

Caesar's supporter and later first governor of Roman Egypt, Cornelius Gallus, wrote a line of poetry about a key river in Ukraine: the Southern Bug, anciently known as Hypanis. It was also described by the historian Herodotus ('Father of lies'). Gallus indicated that the river divided two continents: Europe from Asia. ['*uno tellures diuidit amne duas*', or 'by a single river it divided two lands']. Gallus is remembered for his friendship with the poet Virgil who dedicated his pastoral poem (Eclogue 10) to him, and there we have the first description of Arcadia as a mythical land of peace and tranquillity. Gallus focused on the importance of the Southern Bug River. It has not changed. The port city at the mouth of the river, Mykolaiv (Nikolaev) is being bombed incessantly. It is the gateway for the Russian troops to advance to Odessa. Moreover, behind Odessa is the Russian occupied strip of land, and the self-proclaimed Republic of Transnistria. The Southern Bug is so deep and wide the Germanic tribes could not cross it easily in the early centuries of the Christian era.

Hitler gave Transylvania to Hungary and offered Transnistria to Romania in 1941. That was the region between the Dniester River and the Southern Bug. The region of Transnistria, today an unrecognised republic, hosts the Russian army. If the Southern Bug is crossed by the Russian troops, the next step is Odessa.

The Ukrainians have understood that nature could be their ally. They understood the rivers and generally water are natural obstacles and have threatened to destroy the bridge that connects the Russian mainland to Crimea. Without it, Crimea would be rather isolated. NATO in 1999 bombed the bridges crossing the Danube to subdue Yugoslavia. Putin believes borders are mobile, but the natural obstacles his troops are encountering will not change. The idea that Russia could take over all the land East of the Dnieper and, in the South, reach Odessa with ease, is based on historical precedent, but does not consider the lie of the land. The spring mud, the marshes, and wide rivers could be his quagmire.

15
UKRAINE AND THE THUCYDIDES TRAP

5th August 2022

Thucydides is a great writer and may teach us something about Ukraine. His history of the war between classical Athens and Sparta (431-404bc) is a literary masterpiece. His rendering of Pericles' Funerary Oration, probably the greatest praise of democracy ever written, is stunning. (Thuc. 2.35-46). One may quote his discussion on laws in Athens: *"But while the law secures equal justice to all alike in their private disputes, the claim of excellence is also recognized; and when a citizen is in any way distinguished, he is preferred to the public service, not as a matter of privilege, but as the reward of merit. Neither is poverty a bar, but a man may benefit his country whatever be the obscurity of his condition."* (Thuc. 2.37.1)

The Thucydides trap is a modern expression, employed by Graham T. Allison in an article published in the Financial Times in August 2012, to describe the inevitability of war between great powers. The military build-up of Athens and

Sparta led to war between them. *"The real though unavowed cause I believe to have been the growth of the Athenian power, which terrified the Spartans and forced them into war"* (τὴν μὲν γὰρ ἀληθεστάτην πρόφασιν, ἀφανεστάτην δὲ λόγῳ, τοὺς Ἀθηναίους ἡγοῦμαι μεγάλους γιγνομένους καὶ φόβον παρέχοντας τοῖς Λακεδαιμονίοις ἀναγκάσαι ἐς τὸ πολεμεῖν Thuc. 1.23).

Thucydides got it wrong. He forgot about Persia. He presented the power of Athens as being maritime and then had to explain that the decisive campaigns were by land (Brasidas and Alcibiades). He thought that the Sicilian expedition was the main problem of Athens forgetting the question of Persia. The Comedian Aristophanes made fun of Athenian embassies begging for money at the Persian court already in 427.

The dispute between NATO and Russia is a debate on who can obtain China's support. NATO is a military alliance like that which Athens led, the Delian League. The demise of Athens occurred when one after the other, its allies became neutral or changed sides, out of neglect or frustration. Sparta also headed a military alliance, the Peloponnesian League, whose motto was to go wherever Sparta said by land or sea (ἑπόμενος hόπυι κα Λακεδαιμόνιοι hαγίονται καὶ κατὰ γᾶν καὶ καθάλαθαν *"following wherever the Spartans may lead by land and by sea*"). Russia also seems to be bossing around countries like Belarus or trying with others like Kazakhstan.

Ukraine has become the playground for NATO and Russia. Neither party is interested in this country's welfare. It has been referred to as a proxy war. The aim of both parties may be to make sure China does not colonize Ukraine entirely. If transportation costs rise to an unsustainable level, China will need factories and industries in a country under its control within Europe, to be able to sell its products without long distance transport. NATO and Russia may be offering the entire reconstruction of Ukraine, social and economic, to China. It may be the only country which will be able to foot the bill once the conflicting sides are worn out by unreasonable and pointless military expenses.

China remains the deciding factor. Chinese wealth will tip the balance, like Persian money defined the Spartan victory over Athens in 404 BC. This may not be in China's interest. Within 80 years of the defeat of Athens and the Spartan victory, Persia was conquered by Alexander the Great. As Clausewitz had said, being worn out is the real danger in a war. The Thucydides trap incorrectly points to the inevitability of war, but forgets the political, cultural, and economic void which automatically follows warfare.

16

MASTER AND SLAVE IN FOREIGN AFFAIRS

12ᵗʰ August 2022

We are now living in a class conflict between countries. Small nations are defining the foreign policy of great powers. The tail is wagging the dog. Unfortunately, we do not sit down and think about the dialectic of master and slave. Karl Marx had developed and transformed this notion into the famous 'class conflict', the fight between the bourgeois ruling class and the proletariat, in his Communist Manifesto (1848). He proposed that workers should take over and become rulers. Such a solution was a simplified rendering of Hegel's 'master and slave dialectic'. Leaving philosophical considerations aside, Hegel indicated that the master had lost a sense of ambition, focus, and final aim for his life. The slave, however, had a more fulfilling life by wishing to improve himself. The slave, because he is subordinate to the master, aims to replace him and therefore has a clear goal in life. The slave sublates the master and sees him as a reflection of his better self. *"The master, however, who has interposed the slave between it*

and himself, thereby relates himself merely to the
dependence of the thing [the status quo] and enjoys it
without qualification and without reserve. The aspect of its
independence he leaves to the slave, who labours upon it."
(Hegel Phenomenology of Spirit, 1806)

Small nations are today aiming to include states into their local conflicts to tilt the balance in their favour. They are using their larger allies to achieve their local goals and win over their local foes. World War I and II were particularly terrible also for this reason. Large states found themselves embroiled and entangled in conflicts they could not and wished not to understand. One may think of peoples like the Chechens forming legions within the German army in World War two or of the Sorbian population in Germany, who being Slavic speaking, were considered fellow liberators by the Soviet Union. Such local conflicts are today pushing and defining the policy of those who hold permanent security council seats at the United Nations. The vetoes are often established on a microscopic level. It is a form of proxy diplomacy, led by small nations.

Both Marx and Hegel before him were recalling the original passage on the Master and Slave which is found in Plato's Parmenides. The question there is radically different: if the master is self-sufficient, how can the slave have any contact with him? Marx and Hegel referred knowingly and wittingly to this platonic notion. For Plato being important or even a philosopher means knowing what one is doing and holding the means to achieve it, and therefore being self-sufficient. Society exists only because individuals are not self-sufficient.

It appears that large states are delegating their general direction and policy making to local conflicts. They have abdicated their idea of how society could improve internally and internationally. They should not impose a foreign idea at a local level, but they should not be driven passively by conflicts and warzones, especially if their leaders cannot even place these local events on a map or explain their relevance.

The tail is wagging the dog. Foreign relations are not a game on who controls the outcome, but a form of collaboration negotiated to achieve the best results with the least effort and expense. Diplomacy needs to be defined by results not by egocentric localistic triumphs paraded on television or internet. Results can only come when there is a clearly defined goal.

17
CONSTANTINOPLE CENTRE OF EUROPE AND THE MIDDLE EAST

19ᵗʰ August 2022

E lon Musk reminded us on the 18ᵗʰ June 2022 that Constantinople (and Byzantine culture) is the beating heart of Europe and Middle East. His twitter post was enigmatic and even provoked conspiratorial newspaper headlines, mainly in Turkey, but an indifferent puzzlement elsewhere. The image showed a medieval soldier trying to fall asleep while asking himself if he had left the city gates open. Beneath it reads 'Constantinople, 1453', the year when the Ottoman Turks captured the city and renamed it Istanbul. Musk touched a raw nerve: Constantinople and its legacy.

Most conflicts and complicated areas in Europe and the Middle East have direct or indirect connections with Byzantium. The war in Ukraine is precisely about the legacy of Byzantine culture. The Rus' became Orthodox

Christians when they entered the cultural sphere of the Byzantine Empire, starting with the baptism of their ruler Vladimir/Volodymyr in 988 in Crimea. Ukraine claims to be the rightful heir of this culture which developed around Kyiv, while Russia believes that that same culture was transferred further north and became Muscovy. Moscow calls itself the third Rome, after Rome (Italy), New Rome (Constantinople/Istanbul) since 1448.

The legacy of Byzantine culture is not only central to Ukraine, but also to the Balkans. The innocuous geographic denomination 'Western Balkans' carefully conceals the division, between Catholic and Orthodox, between Latin and Cyrillic alphabets, between Croatia and Serbia, which defined the breakup of Yugoslavia, and which ultimately originate in Constantinople.

The Caucasus is shaped by Byzantine questions. The identity of the Georgian nation and church is defined by its comparison and contrast with Constantinople in the Middle Ages and this feature distinguishes it from both Russia and Armenia, who both focus on other connections with Byzantine culture, creating tensions between the three. Ossetia also has direct links with the Greek speaking

Roman Empire (the first Ossetian inscription is in tenth century Byzantine Greek script).

The Israeli and Palestinian question has important roots in the Byzantine world. Jerusalem was conquered by Arab armies in 638 from the Byzantine Empire. In Syria, the ruling class is composed of members of the Alawite community, who were not recognised as Muslims by the Islamic caliphate and therefore fled in the early 11th century and found refuge in the part of Syria which was under Byzantine control. They are still there as the majority in the area and today form the ruling class of Syria.

The Greek speaking community in Istanbul is the heir of the culture of Constantinople. The head of the Orthodox Church, the Ecumenical Patriarch, is technically archbishop of Constantinople, New Rome. The diplomatic channels opened by the Pope, archbishop of Old Rome (Italy) and Moscow (which refers to itself as the third Rome) are in contrast with the recognition of the Ukrainian Autocephalous Orthodox Church by the Ecumenical Patriarch (Archbishop of the 2nd Rome): more Byzantine tensions.

The central issue is Constantinople. The areas which are diplomatically most complex (Balkans, Ukraine, and Caucasus, as well as the Middle East) derive their cultures from their different legacy with Constantinople for over one thousand years. Many of us would by now be sitting back relieved that Byzantium does not affect us: these are only marginal issues which occur on the news underlined by overzealous journalists or explained by nerdy scholars. We are wrong. Constantinople makes these issues directly relevant to our everyday life. The survival of all classical Greek texts in the original, the backbone of the democratic ideal, European philosophy, and literatures, was due exclusively to Constantinople. It was there that the Roman Law Code was published in 534 (what we call Roman law is effectively a Byzantine code of older Roman laws.). Roman law is studied in China today as a model for future legal reforms.

School memories remind us of Virgil's Aeneid and his description of the flight of Aeneas from Troy, besieged by the Greeks. He took the Palladium, the symbol of his city and brought it to Rome. Caesar had the scene depicted on his coins. Bernini sculpted Aeneas fleeing with his father on his shoulders. The Roman emperor Constantine brought the Palladium to Constantinople, when he founded the city in 330, and placed it at the base of the column today known as the burnt column (Çemberlitaş Sütunu) in Istanbul.

Our mythical legends, apparently imaginary and irrelevant, are real in Constantinople. The distant conflicts which are occupying our headlines prove that Byzantine culture is the pulsing heart of Europe and the Middle East.

18
THE POPE AND DARYA DUGINA

Pope Francis, on 24ᵗʰ August 2022, Ukraine Independence Day, singled out Darya Dugina as an innocent victim of war. The Foreign Minister of Ukraine, Dmytro Kuleba, summoned the Papal Nuncio on 26ᵗʰ August. He gave a formal complaint concerning the Pope's statement. Darya Dugina was killed in a remotely detonated car explosion. The car bomb was the signature weapon of the IRA during the troubles in Northern Ireland. Seán Mac Stíofáin, IRA chief of staff (1969-1972) indicated that the car bomb was a strategic and tactical weapon. Strategically it disrupts government administration and tactically it obliges the enemy forces to concentrate in the area under attack. Moscow has been attacked in a manner well known to the IRA.

So why did Kuleba summon the ambassador and make a formal complaint? The reason was the following statement on the 24ᵗʰ of August during a papal audience in Rome "*I think of that poor girl blown up by a bomb under the seat of her car in Moscow"* the Pope said. *"Innocents pay the price of war, innocents!"* It appears that the Pope and he disagree on what a person is. Pope Francis indicated that Dugina is simply a person, i.e., a person like another. Kuleba has pointed out that the person had political opinions which incited war against the Ukrainians. She had appeared on Russian television supporting the Russian invasion of Ukraine. Her father, Alexander Dugin, has often repeated that Ukraine was not a country and invoked the elimination of the Ukrainian population. It appears that the Pope was indicating that she was simply a victim in war, and her opinions were meaningless. But then why did he single her out on Ukrainian Independence Day, instead of the numerous others who have died in the conflict zone (or other conflict zones)? Kuleba instead indicated that her person could not be separated from her opinions. She was not simply a collection of muscles and bones, but her ideas were an integral part of her as a human.

The argument is centred on the notion of innocence. Pope Francis claimed she was an 'innocent' victim. Innocent derives from a Latin word—innocents—meaning 'which cannot harm'. Dugina was not harmless according to Kuleba. The opinions she held were the reason Russia invaded Ukraine. She did not invent these opinions, nor was she their source or origin but expressed them clearly and therefore perpetuated them publicly. The question that plagues the West is if her father was the origin of these ideas. Did Alexander Dugin's book, 'The Foundations of Geopolitics: The Geopolitical Future of Russia' published in 1997, inspire the opinions within the Kremlin which led to war? Kuleba seems to say that Dugina's opinions caused the invasion of Ukraine. Therefore, she was not innocent. The Pope seems to say, Dugina, was a person with negligible and harmless opinions, and therefore was innocent.

Both agree that she died and how it happened. They disagree on the influence of her opinions —worthless for the Pope and dangerous for Kuleba. Whoever killed her thought her opinions needed to be physically eliminated. The attack was done in a manner which makes no strategic and no tactical sense, according to the definitions of the IRA chief of staff. It may remain a unique event in this war. The problem is that Kuleba has expressed a widely held opinion in Ukraine that Dugina was not innocent. He fulfilled his role as an elected official and represented his constituents by issuing a formal complaint.

The Pope has angered Ukrainian and Eastern European Catholics. He has not pleased the Russian public opinion who see the Jesuits (the Pope is one) and the Catholic Church through the lens of Dostoevsky's 'Grand Inquisitor' (in 'Brothers Karamazov', 1880). He is considered a clear depiction of the West corrupting Russia. This view of the West is the opinion expressed precisely by Darya Dugina.

19

THE POLITICS OF THE UKRAINIAN ALPHABET

7ᵗʰ September 2022

O ne may distinguish Ukrainian and Russian by how they look. Each language has letters which do not occur in the other. Such a phenomenon is due to politics. All Slavic languages which today employ their own version of the Cyrillic alphabet, at one point in the past, used a common alphabet which probably originated in the area of modern-day Bulgaria. The different letters developed to mark different sounds or traditions within each language. Naturally, the history of Ukraine is reflected in its alphabet.

Catholic Austria in 1859 imposed a Latin-based alphabet for Western Ukraine to distance it culturally from the Cyrillic Orthodox world. The Soviet Union wondered what to do with the Ukrainian language. Since 1928, there have been several reforms until the most recent in 2019. The unified spelling for Ukrainian was first established in 1928. When Putin says that Ukraine was Lenin's invention, he is also referring to such an episode. With the 1928 reform, a letter unique to Ukrainian 'ґ' ('g') was standardized. It somehow epitomizes the problem of Ukraine today. The letter was introduced since г is always pronounced as an 'h'. Therefore, Ukrainian has no manner of rendering the sound 'g'. The fluctuation between these two sounds appears in the name of Prague, capital of the Czech Republic (In Czech it is pronounced Praha). Indeed, the pronunciation of 'g' as 'h' is typical of Ukrainian, Slovak, Czech but not Russian, that is, apparently: anyone who has visited St. Petersburg may remember the quarter established by Peter the Great: Nova Gollandia, New Holland. Peter the Great employed 'g' to render the sound 'h'. This fluctuation of 'g' and 'h' was typical in Russian as well, especially before the nineteenth century, and has remained ambiguous today. The German philosopher Hegel is spelled 'Gegel' in Russian today.

The linguistics behind the phenomenon should stay in footnotes. In 1933 however the letter ґ was abolished in another spelling reform which tried to eliminate unique elements of the Ukrainian alphabet. Stalin therefore abandoned his earlier interest in promoting local nationalities and attempted to russify the Ukrainian language. The fact that the same person could hold opposite views within ten years shows how complex the issue is, and how mired in politics it is. The letter ŕ was reintroduced into Ukrainian during yet another spelling reform undertaken during Perestroika years in 1990. Clearly an appeasement for local dynamics which were out of control all over the Soviet Union and led to its breakup.

The Ukrainian alphabet was not the cause of these problems but is an accurate indicator of changed political circumstances. The Ukrainian diaspora in exile outside the Soviet Union used the soviet spelling of 1928 but none of the subsequent ones. The situation was resolved in 2019 when yet another reform was introduced which returned some elements of the 1928 reform, but also accepted subsequent developments. An extraordinary twist of fate is that several words affected by the reform derive from Greek. In Ukrainian there is an ambiguous rendition of Greek terms according to the Latin tradition or the Byzantine one (favoured by countries with an Orthodox heritage). One may now say anafema or anatema in Ukrainian. The latter option being a new Western and not Russian usage. This is not just a Ukrainian problem. It even touches on the word 'European' (ultimately derived from Greek). When one pronounces it as Evropa one uses the old Orthodox form usual in Eastern Europe (Turkish also has Avrupa), while Europa is used in the West. The same division is found between Croatian and Serbian: Europa in Croatian and Evropa in Serbian. This is not pointlessly insignificant. The Bulgarian government blocked an agreement between the EU and Montenegro in 2007 because it insisted that the Euro be referred to as Evro. The entire European Union was held at ransom over this spelling issue by Bulgaria. It is a question of identity. Stalin understood that the presence or absence of certain letters in the Ukrainian alphabet is a matter of national identity. If you eliminate the letter ґ you are eliminating a Ukrainian specificity. The use of the letter was forbidden from 1933 to 1990 in the Soviet Union.

Both Russian and Ukrainian are Eastern Slavic languages. Russian imported south Slavic words into its vocabulary. This veneer of antiquity did not affect Ukrainian in the same way. The word 'grad' (typical of south Slavic languages) 'city' in many city names should be 'gorod'. One may think of Novgorod ('the new city'), as opposed to Stalingrad ('the city of Stalin'). The presidents of Russia and Ukraine share the same first name but spelled differently: Vladimir (South Slavic form used in Russian) and Volodymyr (Ukrainian usage reflecting Eastern Slavic linguistics).

The Ukrainian language allows one to reflect on a problem which Western Europe has forgotten: languages have meaning. In Eastern Europe, language has become a symbol of nationality. This has generated the most bizarre phenomenon visible on Bosnian cigarette packages. The phrase 'smoking kills' is repeated three times on each packet: twice in the Latin alphabet and once in Cyrillic (pušenje ubija, pušenje ubija, пушење убија). Though the spelling and the phrases are identical, they reflect three different constituent nations of Bosnia: Croatian, Bosnian, and Serbian and their respective languages. Overlooking languages and their meaning will condemn us to missing political issues as they emerge and to discover them when it is too late.

20

THE END OF THE BLACK SEA FLEET?

14th September 2022

Putin is facing the possibility of defeat in Ukraine. It could mean Russia's loss of Crimea. While he has been arguing that Crimea is naturally Russian, it was not part of the Russian Empire until 1783. In that year, the city of Sebastopol was established by Potemkin, and the Black Sea Fleet (Черноморский флот) began.

By 2023, he risks losing Crimea, the Sea of Azov and therefore the naval bases in which the fleet was established and set. Indeed before 2014, when Russia annexed the peninsula, the Black Sea Fleet rented its naval base from the Ukrainian State. Both countries had signed a partition treaty of 1997 by which the Soviet Black Sea fleet was divided between Russia (87 percent) and Ukraine (13 percent). The unequal division was compensated by rent paid by Russia to Ukraine for the base at Sebastopol. This rent was used to lower the price of Russian gas to Ukraine. The lease was meant to end in 2017, then an agreement (the Kharkiv Pact) signed on the 21st of April 2010 assured that the lease would continue until 2042. It was signed by President Dmitri Medvedev of the Russian Federation and Viktor Yanukovych of Ukraine (later ousted in the Euromaidan protests of 2014). The numerous agreements between Ukraine and Russia on this complex matter came to an end with the annexation of Crimea and the vote in the Russian parliament (State Duma) on 31st March 2014, making them void and null. If Ukraine takes Crimea, the Black Sea Fleet will be terminated.

The Baltic is now a NATO lake. With the removal of the Black Sea Fleet, Russia would no longer have any voice in the Mediterranean. The Turkish Straits would not need to be international waters (a provision designed specifically for the Soviet Union). Syria would no longer have any support from the Russian navy. The Mediterranean would become a NATO lake as well. The possibility is an upheaval.

The Russian navy has an important revolutionary aspect. The navy stationed on the island of Kronstadt (near Saint Petersburg) was part of the demonstrations in 1905 and 1906 and the revolution of February/March 1917. The working-class sailors rebelled against the noble officers. They also contributed to the Soviet fight against the white-

Russian counter revolution. In 1921 they changed sides, fought against the Soviet government, and were defeated. The navy voiced concerns about food-shortages, freedom of the press, and limitations to demonstrate public dissent. The navy has lost two key operational areas: the Baltic Fleet is locked in Saint Petersburg and Kronstadt (and Kaliningrad). The Black Sea Fleet may simply cease to exist if Crimea becomes Ukrainian.

In all societies the armed forces allow the interaction between people of different backgrounds and ambitions. It is not a social melting pot, but a place where society's concerns often emerge. The sailors of Kronstadt famously paid with their lives their worries about day-to-day life. Putin may have forever lost Crimea to Russia and, in the process, he may have also terminated the Black Sea fleet.

21

UKRAINE VS RUSSIA. THE FINAL BATTLE FOR THE PAST LEGACY

26ᵗʰ September 2022

The war between Ukraine and Russia is about history. It is not about politics or economics. Both countries claim to the rightful heirs of the culture of Rus', the medieval nation whose capital was Kiev/Kyiv. The city became prominent under Viking rulers, the Rurikids, whose dynasty was succeeded by the Romanovs in 1613, in turn overturned by the Soviet revolution of 1917. Saint Vladimir/Volodymyr, first Christian ruler of Rus', was baptised in Crimea in 988 and the family symbol was the trident which is now the state symbol of Ukraine. The church with dazzling mosaics built in the 11th century, Saint Sophia of Kiev/Kyiv, is a striking witness to this glorious past.

The issue arises today from this legacy. The history of Ukraine and Russia went different paths at a certain point. Is Ukraine the rightful heir or is it the Russia Federation?

The reason it is difficult to establish a simple answer is due to the Mongol invasions in 1223. The arrival of the Mongols in Kiev/Kyiv meant some of the leaders moved to other areas and claimed to be the continuation of this culture of Rus'. The key religious position was that of Archbishop of Kiev whose ultimate residence became Moscow and where his title became Metropolitan of Moscow after 1448. Russia invaded Ukraine since it believes all the lands associated with ancient Rus' should be ruled from Moscow (Belarus and Ukraine, among others). Ukraine is resisting since it thinks the culture of Rus' is first connected with the city of Kyiv alone. It is because of history that there are laws limiting the instruction of the Ukrainian language in Russia and of Russian in Ukraine. It is for this reason that there are two main Orthodox churches in Ukraine: one dependent on the Patriarch of Moscow and other lead by the Metropolitan of Kyiv. Putin's invasion of Ukraine has forced both sides to be clear. The category which is abandoned by both sides are the mixed families. Ukrainians and Russians used to be close, their animosities notwithstanding, famously underlined by Solzhenitsyn. Couples were also formed by a Ukrainian and a Russian, their children would be half-Ukrainian and half Russian, and many used to have two passports.

The solidarity shown by Eastern European countries is remarkable but represents a form of empathy which has temporarily put aside historic differences. Ukrainians are Orthodox Christians who use the Cyrillic alphabet. This is different from Poles who are Catholic and write with the Latin alphabet. These differences are also historical and demonstrate that history is far more important than politics or the economy. The temporary alignment in support of Ukrainians does not automatically imply the end of differences between Eastern Europe and Ukraine. The Russians are looking at the area with maps dating from the end of the 18th century when Potemkin established new cities and when the region of Novorossiya was created (the name to be used for the new areas annexed to the Russian Federation) and included in the Russian Empire. The Ukrainians and Poles are focusing more on the 17th century when the two countries were part of the Grand Duchy of Lithuania. This is not a footnote. In 2005 Putin moved the holiday which commemorated October revolution (7th November) to the 4th of November creating the 'Unity Day'. The holiday commemorates the time when a popular uprising in Russia expelled the Polish troops in 1612. The event is commemorated in a sculpture present on Red Square (Monument to Minin and Pozharsky 1818).

History has motivated actions which make no economic or political sense. The battleground today is Ukraine.

22

ADMIRAL TOGO AND UKRAINE

7th October 2022

In Venice to say 'cool' one says 'che Togo'. This is a remarkable tribute to an admiral of the Japanese fleet, Tōgō Heihachirō (1848-1934). He has become proverbial in Venetian dialect because of the Russo-Japanese war 1904-1905. On this occasion, the Russian Baltic fleet circumnavigated the world to reach Japan and found itself exhausted even before starting the war. Togo, as commander in chief of the combined forces, defeated the Russian fleet in 1904 at Port Arthur and then the Baltic fleet at the Battle of Tsushima on 27th– 28th of May 1905. The war was important since it marked the beginning of Japanese expansion in the East. Korea became Japanese that year and remained so until 1945. The peace treatise between Russia and Japan was supervised by Theodore Roosevelt. In the Natural History Museum in New York one can see the fresco showing the signature of the peace treaty. It was then that the USA obtained Panama.

Japan and Russia have had a border dispute over the Kuril Islands. They were offered to the Soviet Union at the Yalta conference on condition that the Soviet Union would declare war on the Japanese Empire. It declared war and invaded the Southern Kuril Islands on 18th -31st August 1945. In 1946, it expelled the entire Japanese population from the islands. On the 7th October 2022, by resolution 2662-IX, the Verkhovna Rada (Ukrainian Parliament) has voted to declare the southern Kuril Islands (Habomai and Shikotan Islands) as unlawfully occupied territory belonging to Japan.

It is an intriguing psychological move. It will sound bizarre in the West and to most NATO allies. However, it will have resonance in Finland. The last time Japan owned the Kuril Islands, Finland owned the city of Vyborg (Viipuri, in Finnish). The Finnish independence movement took strength in the aftermath of the Russo-Japanese war of 1905. Many areas in Russia had uprisings and resulted in the Tsar creating a parliament (the Duma) and offering other concessions. Poland was also part of the Russian empire at the time and remembers the uprising of 1905.

The Russian military defeat on the battlefield resulted in revolution and reform. The Ukrainian parliament is reminding countries which were formally subject to

Russia, and which border with Russia today, that the future is the revolution of 1905.

The year of 1905 was so immense in the public mind that it became proverbial even in the Venetian dialect and remains so even today: che Togo!

23

HOLY WAR IN UKRAINE

18ᵗʰ November 2022

P utin has declared on the 30ᵗʰ September 2022 that the West was practising 'pure satanism'. Medvedev on the 4ᵗʰ of November claimed the 'special operation' in Ukraine is a Holy War. That same day, Alexander Dugin referred to the war as 'the final apocalyptic battle against the Antichrist'. On the 15ᵗʰ October there was a mass shooting at a recruitment office in Soloti, Valuysky District, Belgorod Oblast, Russia. Three Tajiks said that the operation was not a Holy War since, according to Islam, it can only be between Muslims and infidels, while Lt. Lapin had claimed that the special operation was a Holy War. Thirty people died in the shooting which emerged from the disagreement of what is a Holy War.

Putin and Medvedev are Orthodox Christians. Their belief is that Moscow represents the third Rome and is the heir of Ancient Rome and New Rome, Constantinople. The latter was the capital of the Byzantine Empire and the source of Christian belief and practice for Orthodox Christians. One of the preeminent saints and church fathers of the Orthodox Church, Saint Basil, wrote a rule (canon 13) that said that priests could not fight in battle or war. It is for this rule that Anna Comnena (1083-1153), the daughter of the Byzantine emperor, looked in horror at the western practice of priests fighting during the first Crusade (1096-1099):

"For the rules concerning priests are not the same among the Latins as they are with us; For we are given the command by the canonical laws and the teaching of the Gospel, 'Touch not, taste not, handle not! For thou art consecrated'. Whereas the Latin barbarian will simultaneously handle divine things, and wear his shield on his left arm, and hold his spear in his right hand, and at one and the same time he communicates the body and blood of God, and looks murderously and becomes 'a man of blood,' as it says in the psalm of David. For this barbarian race is no less devoted to sacred things than it is to war. And so, this man of violence rather than priest, wore his priestly garb while he handled the oar and had an eye equally to naval or land warfare, fighting simultaneously with the sea and with men". (Anna Comnena *Alexiad* 10.5)

A priest cannot fight according to Orthodox Christianity since there is nothing holy in war. This has been a tradition since the 4th century, for over 1600 years. Putin and Medvedev do not seem to know or understand that war cannot be holy. Even patriarch Kirill of Moscow has had to admit that 'war cannot be holy'. Those who are consecrated cannot participate or endorse war. The Byzantines did not have the notion of 'just war' which originated in the writings of Saint Augustin, a Western, Latin and chiefly Catholic saint. The reason the Byzantines could hold such an opinion is that they believed that war was the realm of the secular world, not of personal belief and faith. It is a tragic outcome of political interaction between humans and societies, and nothing to do with the divine or the afterlife. They basically thought of war as the continuation of political interaction by other means, as Clausewitz said in 1832.

Medvedev has also indicated that the special operation is a holy war against Satan. He stated on the 4th of November that the aim was to *"stop the supreme ruler of hell, whatever name he uses -- Satan, Lucifer, or Iblis"*. He has claimed that each official religion in the Russian Federation identifies the same object with different names. This notion is known as structuralism and interprets each religion as a different expression for the same being. This is a notion which originated in the West and was also typical of Soviet thought about religion. It seems that Putin, Medvedev, and Dugin are expressing their longing to (ab)use western categories of thought which are unknown in traditional Orthodox thought.

Indeed, the special operation is not only a form of intellectual disregard of Orthodox belief but has become an attack against fellow Orthodox Christians (the Ukrainians). The permanent reference to the Satanist West led by Anglo Saxons is disguising the fact that Orthodoxy is fundamentally in favour of peace (like many religions) and that one of the countries in favour of defending Ukraine, the United Kingdom is led by a Hindu, Rishi Sunak.

24

CRIMEA A DEFENCELESS MYTH

6ᵗʰ January 2023

Crimea is a mythical land which cannot be defended. The Russian forces took it in less than a week in 2014 (27ᵗʰ February – 1ˢᵗ March). They had a similar experience in World War Two. They entered Crimea on the 8ᵗʰ of April 1944, and, by the 12ᵗʰ of May, the last German troops had been defeated. The German Army had entered Crimea on the 26ᵗʰ of September 1941, and conquered most of the peninsula by the 30ᵗʰ of October with the main exception of Sebastopol. The peninsula was conquered in less than a month on three separate occasions in the last 75 years. The General who described the German conquest, Erich von Manstein, indicated that any invasion there relies heavily on air support as well as naval help. In other words, once an air force has struck, nothing blocks infantry from entering the peninsula. It is defenceless. The various communities which have historically lived separately within Crimea (Armenians, Greeks, Tatars, among many others) reveal that each group lived its own life relatively undisturbed by history. The lie of the land cannot be changed.

The military strategists even today only want Sebastopol. It is an extraordinary port on the southwest tip of the peninsula which the Soviet Union defended during an incredible eight-month siege in 1941-1942. It was awarded the title of 'hero city'. Potemkin in 1783 established it and then the Russian empress Catherine the Great visited it in 1787 together with the Austrian Emperor Leopold. The site is extraordinary and was built beside the Ancient Greek colony of Chersonesus founded in the 6th century BC. It is a deep-water port, something unusual in that part of the Black Sea. It is a tribute to the accurate eye of the Ancient Greeks who found and colonised it.

It is the symbolic prize of the war between Russia and Ukraine. It is also an extraordinary waste of resources. The Russian Federation was having serious administrative problems as well and economic difficulties with the supply chain before the 24th February 2022. Tensions at a local level were rising. The peninsula is expensive to manage. The key to administer Crimea is a firm control of the regions which border it. They are now battle zones (Cherson, Mariupol, to name just two). Over the centuries this has been an area run over by many different peoples.

The Crimea was less affected by the radical changes than the mainland. The symbolism is due to the ancient Greek civilization: Euripides' Iphigenia in Tauris (5th century BC) is set there, as well as Goethe's Iphigenia auf Tauris (1787). More importantly the first Christian leader of Rus' (Volodymyr/Vladimir) was baptised there in 988. Crimea was part of the Roman Empire from 63 BC (more or less) until the fall of the last Byzantine outpost in Theodoro (Mangup) in 1475. It was Roman for 1538 years. Rome itself fell to invaders in 476 (1200 years after its foundation). Crimea was part of the Roman state longer than Rome itself. This paradoxical statement reveals the mythological status that Crimea has for Russia and Ukraine. From their point of view, it is second only to Constantinople itself, the centre of Roman/Byzantine culture and the centre of Orthodox beliefs.

Crimea is something more relaxed: it has Greek-like beaches, enchanting vineyards, and lovely weather. It is truly a tourist haven, but manifestly a military trap.

25
DID PUTIN FORGET HIS RUSSIAN?

26ᵗʰ April 2023

P utin does not know Russian. His law of 28ᵗʰ February 2023 on 'The administrative language of the Russian Federation' reveals a fundamental problem in the Kremlin. He has signed a law which limits the use of foreign words, words which are not part of the 'Russian literary language'.

Russian is full of foreign words. Indeed, the law itself has at least 150 foreign origin words out of the total 864 words. That is 17 percent of the document is culturally illegal. The main foreign word repeated in the document of Federatsiya. It has become a Russian word, but it is originally Latin, and then it entered Russian via French. Many words in the document have such a path: federalnyi, informatsiya, kommissiya, kvalifikatsiya, lingvistichevkoy, literaturnyi, natsionalnyi, netsensurnyi, norma, normativnich, ofitsialnyi, redaktsiya, registratsiya, territoriya. Several words are easy to recognise since they are like English ones. Other words instead originate from Greek and either come via French or German or Church

Slavonic into Russian: analog, grammatika, organ, sfera, sistema, tehnicheskoi, tekhnologiya, telegramma, tip. There are also words which come either from French or German: resurs, punkt.

Putin has signed a law and demonstrated that he has not understood what two giants of Russian literature did and explained. The first, Pushkin (1799-1837), is credited with importing into Russian words from other Slavic languages, namely South Slavic languages (Russian is an East Slavic language together with Ukrainian!). The clearest case is the word for city in Russian is gorod. In compounds, Russian uses the South Slavic (not Russian) form 'grad': Leningrad, Stalingrad, Volgograd. One notable exception is Novgorod which has the correct and ancient Old Russian form. The name Vladimir is the southern form of Volodymyr, still found in Ukrainian. Indeed, Pushkin introduced numerous foreign south Slavic words into literary Russian. Ukrainian did not; that is one of the differences between the languages.

The second author is the chief witness to this revolution was Griboyedov in his 'Woe from Wit' of 1823. One of the characters of the comedy Famusov is against linguistic innovations. An example of this is the term sudarynya employed in the first scene. This was an old-fashioned term which was replaced by madame. The main character of the play, Chatski, reveals why Putin's law on language purity is bizarre (Griboyedov, *Woe from Wit*, act 3 scene 22):

Воскреснемъ ли когда отъ чужевластья модъ?
Чтобъ умный, бодрый нашъ народъ (615)
Хотя по языку насъ не считалъ за нѣмцевъ.
„Какъ европейское поставить въ параллель
 Съ національнымъ — странно что-то!
„Ну, какъ перевести мадамъ и мадмуазель?
„Ужли сударыня!!" — забормоталъ мнѣ кто-то... (620)
 Вообразите, тутъ у всѣхъ
 На мой же счетъ поднялся смѣхъ.
„Сударыня! ха! ха! ха! ха! прекрасно!
„Сударыня! ха! ха! ха! ха! ужасно!!"

Will we emerge from foreign fashion?
In order that our clever and happy people,
At least in our language, do not consider us Germans.
How to put something European in another way
using national expressions? It is something strange.
Now, how does one translate madame and mademoiselle?
There is sudarynya already, someone started to mutter to me.
Imagine here: among everyone
Laughter arose at my expense.
Sudarynya! Ha! Ha! Ha! Ha! Lovely!
Sudarynya! Ha! Ha! Ha! Ha! Terrible!

The law signed by Putin reasonably excludes those words which have no equivalent in Russian. The term employed is izklyuchat ('exclude') which is a calque of French exclure or German ausschliessen also a calque from Latin excludo. Words, which are not foreign loanwords, are calques from Greek due to the importation of words from Church Slavonic, a language modelled on Greek word formations but using Slavic roots. One more detail: the alphabet used in Russian is also foreign. It is a Greek alphabet adapted to Old Bulgarian and/or Church Slavonic. If one removed the foreign elements from the law Putin has signed, little would be left, and it would not be applicable.

As Griboyedov brilliantly said: how does one put something European in national terms? Not with a law which does not solve the problem, but which makes it emerge. The first word which should be banned by this law is the Russian президент—'president'—which is borrowed from French and Latin.

26

BELGOROD

23ʳᵈ May 2023

On the 22ⁿᵈ of May 2023 Russia was invaded. By whom and for what is not clear. It is a sort of Special Operation, such as the Russians undertook on 24ᵗʰ February 2022. No war declaration. Unfortunately, a year and half ago the Russian Federation has effectively thrown international law to the wind and declared that border posts represent nothing. They can be removed and crossed. The Freedom of Russia Legion, who has undertaken the latest military incursion, claims their final aim is Red Square in Moscow. This statement is in Russian, and many western journalists and commentators seem unaware of this goal. This somehow summarized the problem. Russia is the enemy in the West, though little known.

The real question one should ask is: Is this the first invasion? The Russian Federation was created in 1917 after the October Revolution. Before that date, the Russian empire was administered differently. So, the starting point is 1917. During the Polish Soviet war, the Russian Federation was not affected. It was Byelorussia/Bielorus which was invaded. The same with Operation Barbarossa in 1941. The first time, the Germans entered the Russian Soviet Socialist Republic after a few weeks of invading the USSR.

Indeed Leningrad, Moscow and Stalingrad (now Volgograd) were famously under siege by the German and Axis armies. Since their defeat Russia has not had foreign troops until the 22nd May 2023, when the Russia Freedom Legion launched an attack towards Belgorod.

Given that the Ukraine conflict appears to be a proxy war on all sides, we can leave aside who is behind it. The question is who this Freedom of Russia is Legion. If it is a Russian freedom fighting formation, as claimed by the West, then it indicates that the Russian Federation is imploding and explains why so many private military companies (PMC) are being formed (including some under the control of Gazprom). If it is a foreign invasion, as the Russians claim, then it means that the West thinks the Federation cannot defend itself and may implode.

Ironically, similar considerations set the Russian Special Operation into motion last year. The Kremlin believed that, with a little push, the Kyiv government would collapse. The West somehow agreed and decided to support

Zelensky's defence effort. Who will help Russia, if it is under the same scenario?

27
WOMEN'S PROTESTS IN RUSSIA

5th June 2023

W omen's political protests are often far more significant than men's ones. On the 26th of May 2023, the Ministry of Justice of the Russian Federation stated that the Council of Mother's and Wives (Совет матерей и жен) represents foreign agents. Such an act constitutes the recognition by Russian authorities that, if women's voices are heard and their protests seen, civil society will take note. Leaving aside the social reasons for such an attitude and such a reaction, the fact speaks for itself: when women protest, there is concrete trouble.

The Tsarist regime fell because of the March Revolution of 1917 begun by mothers and wives asking about their sons and husbands dying at the front during World War one. Their slogan was 'bread and peace'. On the 8th of March (23rd February old calendar) 1917 International Women's Day demonstration in Petrograd gained momentum. Their request was bread and peace. The Tsar abdicated seven days later (15th March 1917). One could argue that the October revolution simply took advantage of the protest and upheaval indicated by women a few months earlier. Many countries celebrate International Women's Day on the 8th of March to remember this event.

Women's protests played a role asking about their male relatives serving for the USSR in Afghanistan in 1989 as they did during the Chechen campaign in 1995. Some could argue that the Afghan war was the straw which broke the back of the USSR leading to its collapse and disintegration. The Chechen war and its failure led to the fall of the Yeltsin presidency which was then replaced by Putin in 1999. There is no point speculating on how central or important women's protests are in each society. Women's protests are a crucial fact in a social upheaval. They identify the actual collapse of a perceived balance within a society.

The Russian government and parliament have accepted this as fact and therefore have silenced eventual protests from the Council of Wives and Women. Putin by this law indicates that if women protest the war in Ukraine, he risks having to handle a revolution at home like 1917 or 1989-1991.

28

DEMOCRACY AND IMPERIALISM
CLASSICAL ATHENS AND NATO

18th June 2023

The freedom of democracy comes at a price: imperialism. This is probably the most striking lesson of the ancient Greek historian Thucydides who gave us the main narrative of events concerning classical Athens in the golden age of democracy (5th century BC).

The health of a democracy is more easily measured by the number of allies. When Athens was winning the Peloponnesian war (431-404) it had numerous allies. They each paid tribute and provided weapons (Athenian Tribute lists). When the tide turned in 413 it only had two: Chios and Mytilene. Allies leave in the face of defeat. Allied support is defined by their participation in the wealth of the alliance's leadership, including economic embargoes. They benefit from the exclusion of commercial competitors defined by the leading country. One of the starting points of the Peloponnesian War was the Megarian Decree, an economic embargo against the city of Megara (book 1). The poverty which struck this city lead some of its citizens to trade illegally as the comic playwright Aristophanes depicts in his play 'The Acharnians' in 427bc.

If a democracy invades another country, allies share some of the gained treasures and wealth. The acquisition of land and territories is part of the democratic process. Allies benefit and often approve when their Alliance subjugates a neighbouring and maybe problematic country. Thucydides describes how the Athenian assembly voted to invade Mytilene and to have the population enslaved or eliminated (Book 3). He also describes the subjugation of Melos, in the infamous Melian dialogue. The delegation voted and sent by Athenian democracy argued that 'might is right' against the defenceless local representatives (Book 5). NATO receives contributions from allies which in turn benefit from wealth acquired by the alliance through military action as well as from embargoes.

The centre of the Alliance was not in Athens but on the island of Delos. One of the reasons was to show equality between allies. It was known as the Delian league. NATO also has its head office in Brussels rather than in Washington DC.

Alliances can also create legal tensions in tribunals. The USA has often and repeatedly been criticised of applying a sort of extraterritoriality for its soldiers, and sometimes also for its citizens. Americans are not prosecuted abroad. Classical Athens did the same. The orator Antiphon, much admired by Thucydides (book 8), used to argue in court cases against those Athenians who could avoid prosecution in allied jurisdictions. He prosecuted a certain Herod, who had killed a citizen of an allied country on the island of Mytilene. He had escaped prosecution locally and was appealing in the court of Athens to avoid condemnation. Antiphon had noticed that a weak point of Athenian democracy was the imbalanced treatment between Athenians and the citizens of allied countries. While allied citizens may not be considered as equals, power is effectively in the hands of the diplomatic corps who negotiates imperial ambitions. This leads to a curious imbalance where internal policy is defined by elected officials while foreign policy is defined by career bureaucrats. Foreign affairs become the stable backbone of an internal open society.

Foreign regime change is also typical of democracy. The comedian Aristophanes made fun of the sale and export of democratic constitutions to other countries in the play the Birds. It is there where the phrase 'cloud cuckoo land' was coined to refer to a new country not subject to the perceived Athenian inequality. There a 'constitution salesman' arrives to provide a ready-made democratic constitution for the new country. He is ridiculed and sent away.

The matter at hand is not the justice of democracy, but the fact that the democratic procedure internal to a country depends on a network of allies and diplomatic relations which are appointed and not elected. There appears a two-world system. Internal debate and external decision making appear in contradiction but are at the very core of democracy also in classical Athens.

The health and strength of a democratic regime (rather than its equality or justice) can thus be measured by counting the number of allies which support it. Athens in 431 was rather healthy as is NATO in 2023.

29

THE BUILDUP TO THE COUP D'ÉTAT IN MOSCOW
KALLIPOLIS' PREDICTIONS OF CURRENT EVENTS

25ᵗʰ June 2023

The following is a selection of articles which predicted the events of the 24ᵗʰ June 2023. The analyses, more than a year old, contained here have found confirmation yesterday. At the end of this article there will be some considerations about probable future scenarios.

The almost coup d'état in Moscow was the result of dissatisfaction with the results of the war in Ukraine.
The main problem is the Russian misunderstanding of Ukraine as pointed out by Solzhenitsyn (Solzhenitsyn on Ukraine 1968 [Chapter 5]) and a misunderstanding of Ukrainian geography (Into the Roadless Land: The Russian invasion of Ukraine [Kallipolis, 27ᵗʰ May 2022]).
The natural barriers have been neglected even if important

in Roman times (Mykolaiv and Roman Poetry [Chapter 14]). The cult of Crimea as a fortress does not stand the test of history. A land difficult to defend and endlessly overrun by invaders (Crimea a defenceless myth [Chapter 24]).

The neglect of the differences between Ukrainian culture and Russian reveals the rather weak understanding of one's own culture (Did Putin forget his Russian? [Chapter 25]) and language (The politics of the Ukrainian Alphabet [Chapter 19])

The Special Operation did not explain the fact that the aim of war is victory whatever the cost, as Clausewitz had pointed out (Clausewitz on Ukraine [Chapter 8]). The price of defeat would be a partition like that seen during the Russian civil war in 1917-1921 (Putin's plan for the partition of Russia [Chapter 13]). Defeat reopens the question of who will control Kaliningrad in the future (All roads lead to Kaliningrad [Chapter 12]).

The parallel with the revolution of March 1917 is important. Russia has banned women groups who protested the current situation. International Women's Day (8th March) celebrates an event in Moscow of 1917 (Women's protests in Russia [Chapter 27])

The breakup of Russia is occurring now not with a dismemberment of the Federation but the creation of paramilitary groups (private military companies, or PMC) which are controlling areas, as if they were medieval fiefdoms. A situation which recalls the breakup of Yugoslavia. (How Russia is outsourcing its war effort to paramilitary groups [Kallipolis 9th May 2023]). The invasion of Belgorod this year is consolidating the importance of PMC as one has seen with Wagner's march towards Moscow yesterday. (Belgorod [Chapter 26])

The NATO reaction was an excellent opportunity for the alliance to test its allies and to fight a proxy war. (Democracy and Imperialism: Classical Athens and NATO [Chapter 28]). NATO has included Finland (A tale of polar diplomacy and suppressed sorrow: The end of an era for Finland and the world [Kallipolis 6th June 2022]) and probably Sweden as well (Swedish neutrality between the Cossacks and Ukraine [Chapter 6]) in its alliance.

China clearly stands to benefit from the conflict from every point of view since the outset of the special operation (Ukraine and the Thucydides Trap [Chapter 15])

One future scenario is that Russia has declared Ukrainian borders as meaningless. Russian defeat will result in redrawing of its borders and concessions (Admiral Togo and Ukraine [Chapter 22]). The only way borders may be redrawn is by a careful analysis history and precedent (Ukraine vs Russia: The final battle for the past legacy [Chapter 21]), remembering that both countries owe their culture and religion from Constantinople (Constantinople, centre of Europe and the Middle East [Chapter 17]).

30
BENGHAZI AND THE FUTURE OF LIBYA

1ˢᵗ July 2023

Who controls Benghazi controls Libya. It is an old unchanging story and crucial to today (given the presence of General Haftar and the Wagner group). When the Italians invaded Libya in 1911, they took control of the Western half of it within a year. The area was formerly called Tripolitania and centred around Tripoli, the capital of the country to this day. The other, Eastern half took them almost twenty years to subdue and was never managed. By the early 1940s, it was the site of fierce fighting between Axis and Allies which culminated symbolically with the battle of El-Alamein. The headquarters of German general Erwin Rommel, for part of this time where in Tobruk, also in the Eastern area of Libya.

Libya is effectively divided into two distinct areas. Contemporary commentators muddy the waters by indicating the numerous tribes which inhabit Libya, not for the benefit or understanding of the reader. Geographically, there is Tripolitania to the West and Cyrenaica to the East. The division of the two areas in antiquity was linguistic and cultural. The west was Latin speaking while the East was Greek speaking. When the Roman empire was divided in 395, Tripolitania fell in the Western half, while Cyrenaica was in the East. The cultural divide is immense. It is the divide which runs through the middle of Bosnia as well. The west of Libya is characterized by Roman archaeological sites which show syncretic culture with the local populations. The great site of Lepcis Magna may also be spelled Leptis Magna since the word is not Latin but of a local Punic (Phoenician) language. The East has the great site of Cyrene, an ancient Greek colony of the island of Thera (Santorini). It is described by Herodotus (the Father of History) and praised by Pindar (the great poet) both in the 5th century BC. It was the centre of a great mathematical School and the chief temple dedicated to Zeus was probably the model of the Parthenon on Athens' Acropolis. Plato's dialogues Theaetetus, Sophist, and Statesman had as a main interlocutor Theodore of Cyrene.

Cyrenaica was Greek, hilly, and fertile. Tripolitania was a Latin speaking desert.

The Ancient Egyptians had strong connections with Cyrenaica. This is also geographic since a caravan route from central Egypt would go through Siwa oasis (where

120

Alexander the Great was recognized as a God) and continue to Cyrene.

Even in Ancient Egyptian hieroglyphs Libya was Tehenu (⸘⸙⸚) but referred only to Cyrenaica. This was already attested in ca 3200 BC (king Scorpio of Egypt). The city which is in between Tripolitania and Cyrenaica is Sirte which is where Ghaddafi came from. He was a compromise of East and West Libya and thus managed to control them both with an iron fist. However, Egypt and the wider Nile valley will always be allied with Eastern Libya, while Tunisia and Algeria will try to establish connections with Tripolitania.

The future of Libya is either a division into two countries or a balance between Benghazi and Tripoli. But whoever controls Benghazi will have the upper hand, geographically, militarily, and maybe even politically.

31

THE DECISION-MAKER AND ANALYST PARADOX

7th *July 2023*

Those who decide do not analyse. Those who analyse do not decide. Today's paradox is before everyone's eyes: responsibility. Indeed, decision makers are not accountable for the quality of the decision they take, while analysts are not responsible for their opinions.

No one cares how good or bad an outcome is, if someone analyses and someone else decides. This is why we enjoy claiming that Plato's Republic is a Utopia, a fantasy Never-Land. He lived in a parliamentary democracy, regularly renewed by elections. His book, The Republic, reveals his concern of his everyday worries, not only of his philosophical aspirations.

If we replace the term king with decision maker and philosopher with analyst, his Republic (book 5, 473) reads like a punch in the stomach in passages such as these (in bold are the replaced words):

"But say it I will, even if, to keep the figure, it is likely to wash us away on billows of laughter and scorn. Listen." "I am all attention," he said.
*"Unless," said I, "either **analysts** become **decision makers** in our states or those whom we now call our **decision makers** and rulers take to the pursuit of analysis seriously and adequately, and there is a conjunction of these two things, decision and analysis, while the motley horde of the natures who at present pursue either apart from the other are compulsorily excluded, there can be no cessation of troubles, dear Glaucon, for our states, nor, I fancy, for the human race either. (adapted translation)*

Corruption and decline, for Plato, are defined by the separation of analysis and decision.

Plato is an ancient author, but his ideas are new and permeate our language. The term 'government' comes from 'governor' itself from Latin *gubernator*, which is an old transliteration of κυβερνήτης (*kybernetes*) [which gives us also cybernetic] which indicates the person who steers a ship. The governor is technically the helmsman. In ancient Egyptian thought it was the Sun God (Horus) who steered the dead pharaoh in the afterlife (according to the

Amduat). It was Plato (pace Alceus) who gave real meaning to the 'governor' not as the ruler of a ship but of a political establishment, in his Republic (Book 6, 488a–489d). There he points out that the captain, the gubernator, is rather aloof and abstract, while the sailors want to overthrow him since they want to decide without his training and understanding. The ship of state is an image which points out how every part of society needs to respect and collaborate with the other, lest the ship sink.

Analysis and decision need to be combined, as Plato indicates in the ship of state (government) as well as his idea of the philosopher kings, which are decision makers who think before they act. The paradox is: think, before you act, and assume responsibility.

32

Secularism to mystic fanaticism in the French Revolution

14th July 2023

During the Reign of Terror (1793-1794), secularism became a form of mystic fanaticism. This was the reason for which Robespierre, the Terror's protagonist, was deposed in 1794. Secularism (Fr. *laïcité*) is a central contribution of France. It is the separation between religion and politics or rather the restriction of religion to the private and individual sphere. Beliefs are not meant to affect society. It has become an ideal for many political parties worldwide and plays a significant role, among others, in Turkey's constitution, considered by some the most secular in the world (even more than France).

Article 4 of the Declaration of the Rights of Man and the Citizen of 1789 introduced the notion of secularism into French law. The Constitution of France today includes this text. The Declaration of the Rights of Man and the Citizen, as published on the 20th of August 1789, has the following preamble.

« En conséquence, l'Assemblée nationale reconnaît et déclare, en présence et sous les auspices de l'Être suprême, les droits suivants de l'homme et du citoyen. »

Therefore, the National Assembly recognizes and declares, before and under the auspices of the Supreme Being the following rights of man and of the citizen.

The principle is metaphysical and religious. French secularism was then marked by its transformation into the cult of the Supreme Being (*culte de l'être Suprême*). It had its own priesthood, temples, baptism, and rites. The painter Jacques-Louis David choreographed the feast of the cult of Supreme Being on the 8th of June 1794. Philosophically the notion of Supreme Being is rather peculiar. Plato had said the Divine was beyond being, though Aristotle and Thomas Aquinas would probably agree with the notion of Supreme Being.

On the 15th of June 1794, Vadier, president of the Committee of National Safety, revealed the existence of a conspiracy aimed at destabilising the Revolution. His act of accusation read before the Assembly is extraordinary. Vadier claimed that Catherine Theot had declared herself as a priestess of the cult of the Supreme Being. She was a *"New Eve"*. She was also the *"Mother of God"*. Apparently, the biblical prophets Ezekiel and Isaiah had predicted the arrival of Robespierre as a Messiah, a Saviour who would console the poor. Vadier had also found several cabalistic tracts and amulets during the perquisition of her meeting place at Place de la Contrescarpe, as well as a painting of the son of Louis XVI and Marie Antoinette, by Vigée Lebrun. Theot is an interesting case, since she had also been considered a prophetess before the revolution and had been consulted by the Duchess of Bourbon [whose palace in Paris is now the National Assembly]. Robespierre was implicated in the 'Affaire Theot' and executed on the 28th of July 1794. It was the end of the Reign of Terror and of the French Revolution. The fate of the reign of Terror was thus forever associated with secularism and its fanatical mystical degeneration.

The control of religion in society was dependent on the Committee of Public Safety under the direction of Vadier. The event reveals a contradiction of such a form of secularism, in which a committee must supervise the interference of private belief in society. The key to this episode is Vadier, whose name has been forgotten since he sided with Babeuf against Napoleon, and therefore has become a footnote of history ever since 1796. He is buried beside the painter David in Brussels, both exiled, both connected with the Cult of the Supreme Being and the Prophetess Catherine Theot, the revolutionary mystic of the cult of the Supreme Being.

33

THE GLASS CURTAIN
GOTHIC EAST AND WEST

21ˢᵗ July 2023

I t is not an Iron Curtain which divides Europe, but a glass one. We could cross, but we only look through it. There are numerous ways of defining the mutual misunderstanding, which is casting a long shadow over Europe today. West of Poland, nations wish to create a restricted club of like-minded G7 members within the EU. East of Germany, countries are defined by rapid economic growth, improving opportunities, and a common mistrust of Russia's presence in Ukraine. This ancient divide runs along the Oder River and the Neisse River down to Trieste. It marked the furthest expansion of the Mongol Empire in 1241 (battle of Legnica/Leignitz). Today it divides Germany and Poland. However, it is even older and divides the peoples who spoke Germanic languages. It is useless, even if apparently comfortable, to say that it separates different peoples. The proof lies in the influence of the Goths, a Germanic people, on today's languages.

The Goths moved from the area of Prussia (North East Poland, Kaliningrad Oblast, South West Lithuania) around the 2nd century AD. They migrated towards Romania, Greece, the Western Balkans until they took over the Western Roman Empire creating the Kingdom of Italy in 476. They migrated, settled, and assimilated.

Their language was an Eastern Germanic language (now extinct). English, Dutch and German are Western Germanic. Norwegian, Swedish are Northern Germanic languages.

Gothic gave the word for bread to all Slavic languages: hleb (Old Slavonic хлѣбъ) derives from Gothic 𐌷𐌻𐌰𐌹𐍆𐍃 (hlaifs). Western Germanic people use words like 'bread' (Brot in German). Gothic gave the word for glass to all Slavic languages. Sklo (Old East Slavic стькло) refers to glass and comes from Gothic 𐍃𐍄𐌹𐌺𐌻𐍃 (stikls). The term appears in all Slavic languages, Lithuanian, Latvian, as well as Romanian (and Old Prussian). The Western Germanic languages use 'glass' (German glas). Gothic was also spoken in Crimea in the form Crimean Gothic, possibly until 1945.

If one places on a map the countries which have this common Gothic vocabulary, one has an almost overlap of the Polish Lithuanian Commonwealth (1569-1795) and more recently the group of countries called the Three Seas Initiative (begun in 2015).

The Goths in their migration went West and left important traces in Italy, France, Spain and Portugal. The word 'ambassador' derives from the Gothic notion of serving the king (ᚨᚾᛊᛒᚨᚺᛏᛁ andbahti 'service') and the term feudalism derives from a term such as fehu (ᚠᚨᛁᚺᚢ cattle in Gothic). The relation with the monarchy gave many first names with gothic etymologies, especially in Spain and Portugal, where the Goth created a kingdom (first capital Toulouse, then Toledo): Alarico, Alfonso, Alvarado, Amalarico, Froila, Godofredo, Gonzalo, Guzman, Ildefonso, Ramiro, Recaredo, Rodrigo, Rosendo, Velasco, Zamora. Even the French royal name Louis is a Germanic name (Hlōdowik means 'famous in battle' or 'sharing battle'). Charles, Frederick, Richard, Robert, William are also examples of common Germanic names.

The royal and social aspect gave the West the word 'caste' (from Gothic *ᚱᚨᛊᛏᛊ *kasts), defining a stratification of society. The Goths refused Roman Law, which they left to the lower levels of society, while using Germanic law exclusively for their nobility (Code of Euric, Salic law among many others) creating inherited noble titles in the

133

process. The end of Roman law in the West marks the beginning of the Middle Ages, compared to the East which continued to have the influence of Roman law through Constantinople and the Byzantine Empire.

In Italy, the transition from Roman law to the new Gothic legal situation was rather radical. The loanwords indicate violent confrontations: *Astio* = hatred / resentment (gothic 𐌷𐌰𐌹𐍆𐍃𐍄𐍃 *haifsts*, "conflict, strife"); *Bega* = quarrel (gothic *𐌱𐌰𐌹𐌲𐌰 **bega* "fight"); *guardia* = guard (gothic 𐍅𐌰𐍂𐌳𐌾𐌰 *wardja* "keeper"). East of the Oder Neisse Rivers, the Gothic words seem to reflect technological innovations or improvements. When the Goths reached Italy, they brought rather violent words into the late Latin language. In France, Spain, and Portugal the kingdom of the Visigoths brought notions of social class, nobility, and with it the prestige of awarding Gothic first names.

The second century Roman Historian Tacitus refers to a Germanic word 'glas' (latin *glaesum*) as amber. Given that most amber comes from the Curonian and Vistula lagoons, the heartland of the Goths (Prussia), the transformation of the word goblet (𐍃𐍄𐌹𐌺𐌻𐍃 stikls) into glas for the local implies working of the material into objects. King Theodoric of Italy (6th century) wrote a letter (written by his minister Cassiodorus) talking about the amber route from the land of the Aesti (Prussia more or less) and Italy.

Theodoric was a Gothic ruler of Italy from 493 to 526. The amber route gives us literary evidence for the contact of the areas of Italy and Prussia which were under Gothic influence, already ascertained in the languages. Archaeologists refer to this area with the terms Wielbark and Chernyakov cultures. They define the areas to which the Goths migrated to and where they settled.

The Goths are relevant since the geographic extent of the Chernyakov culture corresponds to today's Ukraine.

34
NARENDRA MODI AND BYZANTINE WINE

28ᵗʰ July 2023

The Prime minister of India, Narendra Modi, went to France and celebrated the 14ᵗʰ of July with President Emmanuel Macron. A state banquet followed, during which, Macron raised a toast to the guest. Modi raised the glass of wine but did not drink. He is a teetotaller. Wine is important in France and considered a symbol of socialization. As a Hindu, Modi does not drink alcohol. Such a rule is recorded in numerous Sanskrit texts, but one may single out the Manu Smriti मनुस्मृति a key early Hindu legal code from the early centuries of the Christian Era. Here it describes what is appropriate for the Brahmins:

"There is no sin in the eating of meat, nor in wine, nor in sexual intercourse. Such is the natural way of living beings; but abstention is conducive to great rewards." (Manu Smriti 5:56 Olivelle).

Abstention from Madya मद्य (intoxicating drink) is important. The ancient Greek philosopher Plato in his Laws (4th century BCE) had also recommended that those in charge of society should abstain from wine.

"So, a sober and wise leader must overlook the drunk, rather than the opposite. An unwise, young drunk among drunkards, would be lucky if he did not do a great misdeed." (Plato *Laws* 640d4-7 Burnet)

The great Byzantine Greek epic poem about the War between the God Dionysus and the Indians written in the 5th century AD, talks about Dionysus, the God of Wine. It is the Dionysiaca of Nonnos of Panopolis. It is the same length of Homer's Iliad and Odyssey combined. The poem refers to brahmins, occasionally, but more importantly indicates the Indians as teetotallers. One of the leaders of the Indians says his weapon is his sword rather than wine. The God Dionysius fights the Indians, and their king Deriades, with wine. He even transforms the river Hydaspes (mod. Jhelum in Pakistan) into wine:

"But the god pitied his foes in his heart of merry cheer, and he poured the treasure of wine into the waters. So, he changed the snowy white waters to yellow, and the river swept along bubbling streams of honey intoxicating the waters. When this change came upon the waters, the breezes

blew perfumed by the newly poured wine, the banks were empurpled. A noble Indian drank, and spoke his wonder in these words" (Nonnos *Dionysiaka* 14.411-418)

King Deriades of the Indians refuses wine. He drinks only the pure water of the river Hydaspes (Sanskrit Vitástā वितस्ता):

"I accept no other drink than golden Hydaspes.
My wine is the spear, my potion too the shield!"
(Nonnos *Dionysiaka* 21.259-260)

In the Sanskrit Nilamata Purana, written between the 5th and 10th century AD, the river Hydaspes is called Vitástā वितस्ता (also known as Jhelum) and is also divine for the Hindus as Nonnos claims.

Prime minister Modi of India does not drink alcohol since it is an intoxicating drink. The Byzantines, and specifically Nonnos of Panopolis, were aware of such practices by the Indian ruling class in the 5th century, contemporary with the codification of such ascetic politics in Sanskrit. Indian ideals are accurately described in Byzantine mythological epic poetry.

Is Byzantine culture a privileged European vehicle to understand today's India?

139

35

PUTIN'S DESTRUCTION OF PAN SLAVISM

6ᵗʰ August 2023

Putin's invasion of Ukraine has put an end to the collaboration between Slavic nations. Russia and Ukraine are the two most populous countries which speak Slavic languages. Their conflict puts an end to the pan Slavic idea: the consideration that different nations were connected by the common root of their languages. These are the 'Slavic' countries:

Belarus - 9,498,700
Bosnia & Herzegovina - 3,829,000
Bulgaria - 7,265,000
Croatia - 4,253,000
Czech Republic - 10,200,000
Macedonia - 2,107,000
Montenegro - 621,383
Poland - 38,530,000
Russia - 143,500,000
Serbia - 7,164,000
Slovakia - 5,414,000

Slovenia - 2,060,000
Ukraine - 45,490,000

These countries have languages which are remarkably close and almost mutually understandable. If one translates the word fish into Slavic languages one sees why the pan Slavic idea emerged:

рыба (rýba): Belarussian
риба (ríba): Bulgarian
rȉba: Croatian
ryba: Czech
риба (ríba) Macedonian
рѝба (rȉba): Montenegro
ryba: Polish
рыба (rýba): Russian
рѝба (rȉba): Serbia
ríba: Slovene
риба (rýba): Ukrainian

Romance and Germanic languages cannot compete with such shared vocabulary. The pan Slavic idea considered that nations whose languages were close (much greater than romance languages or even Germanic languages) should consider further collaboration. This is why most Slavic countries have flags with three horizontal stripes, blue, white and red. The pan Slavic flag was introduced at the Slavic Congress of Prague in 1848. The countries considered the Slavic nation more important than religion. Indeed, there are Jewish, Christian, and Muslim Slavs. Moreover, there are two alphabets employed: the Latin and Cyrillic. The pan-Slavic movement overlaps also with the notion of Eurasia, that is the Russian Federation plus the territories of Western and Balkan Slavs.

This pan-Slavic ideal explains an ambiguity in the Kremlin's attitude towards Ukraine. If they accept to be part of Russia, they are brothers, if they reject it, they are against the notion of Slavic and Eurasian Brotherhood and need to be defeated. What is striking is that Ukraine uses the Cyrillic alphabet and are Orthodox Christians like Russia. However, the overarching pan-Slavic, Eurasian idea has destroyed any form of contact or collaboration between Ukraine and the Russian Federation soon. A conflict between two neighbouring countries implies the creation of future artificial trade routes which will avoid the trading partner with which one borders. If Putin loses the war with Ukraine, he will have no trade with a significant neighbouring country. If Ukraine regains control of the territories it had before 2014, Russia will lose important access routes to the Black Sea.

Pan-Slavism, in theory is based on collaboration and friendship. Putin has ended it by invading Ukraine on the 24th of February 2022.

36
CLASSICAL LANGUAGES OF INDIA AND EUROPE

11ᵗʰ August 2023

Europe cannot compete with India in many fields. One of these is classical languages. The Indian government in 2004 established a list of 'classical Indian languages'. These are languages included among the 22 defined in the Indian constitution (schedule eight). Currently, six languages enjoy the 'Classical' status: Tamil (declared in 2004), Sanskrit (2005), Kannada (2008), Telugu (2008), Malayalam (2013), and Odia (2014). The criteria established to include a language into such a privileged elite were described by Ambika Soni (Congress Party) in the Rajya Sabha (Upper House of Indian Parliament) in 2006:

"High antiquity of its early texts/recorded history over a period of 1500–2000 years; a body of ancient literature/texts, which is considered a valuable heritage by generations of speakers; the literary tradition be original

and not borrowed from another speech community; the classical language and literature being distinct from modern, there may also be a discontinuity between the classical language and its later forms or its offshoots."

The Indian parliament examined the twenty-two languages defined by the Indian constitution and has selected six as classical Indian languages. These benefit from a special status and government support.

Europe does not support its classical languages, nor does it give them a special status. If we apply the criteria above to the European continent, then the results are startling. The official languages of the European Union are the following: Bulgarian, Croatian, Czech, Danish, Dutch, English, Estonian, Finnish, French, German, Greek, Hungarian, Irish, Italian, Latvian, Lithuanian, Maltese, Polish, Portuguese, Romanian, Slovak, Slovenian, Spanish and Swedish.

Which European languages fulfil the following criteria established by the Indian Parliament?
1) Recorded for over 1500/2000 years
2) Body of ancient texts
3) Literary tradition

The results are: Greek (recorded since the 16th century BC).

This is highly problematic for Europe today. Languages which are considered significant in the EU, are rather new by Indian standards.

French (Oaths of Strasburg in 842AD; Eulalia Sequence 880AD)

Italian (Verona Riddle 8th/9th century; Placiti Cassinesi 960AD)

Portuguese (Doação à Igreja de Sozello 870AD, Carta de dotação e fundação da Igreja de S. Miguel de Lardosa 882AD)

Spanish (Glossas Emilianenses 10th – 11th century)

The oldest dated Slavic text is a gravestone erected by Tsar Symeon in 993.

Old High German (Abrogans 750AD)

Old Norse (Runic inscriptions 8th century)

Irish (Book of Armagh c. 812)

No spoken language in the European Union (except Greek) has a text older than 750 AD.

If one considers the European continent in its widest sense and includes the shores of the Mediterranean, one would be able to include: Hebrew (10th century BC); Armenian (since 5th century: bible translation); Georgian (since 5th century: Martyrdom of Saint Shushanik the Queen by Jakob Tsurtaveli); Coptic (since the 2/3rd century AD) (if one includes Egypt); Syriac (1st century AD); Arabic is first attested in the early 6th century in Syria. (Zabad 512AD).

However, what is clear is that India promotes the past heritage as a base to construct the future. Europe is progressing forward but leaving its distant past to one side. India protects and promotes its classical languages. According to Indian criteria, only Greek fulfils the criteria of a classical language which should be promoted and protected.

37
ANCIENT INDIAN DEMOCRACY

18ᵗʰ August 2023

The president of India, Droupadi Murmu, praised ancient Indian democracy on the 14th of August 2023, the eve of the 77th anniversary of the Independence of India. She specifically referred to it as precolonial. The colonial era of India is defined thus:

British India 1600–1947
Portuguese India 1505–1961
Dutch India 1605–1825
Danish India 1620–1869
French India 1668–1954
Swedish India 1731–1813
Austrian India 1778–1785

It does not seem to include Moghul India even though the Moghuls represented foreign powers which arrived in India in 1526 lead by Babur, from today's Uzbekistan, and the Sultanate of Delhi (1206-1526) established by Qutb ud-

Din Aibak, a Turkic Mamluk slave-general of the Ghurid Empire from Central Asia. One may take 1206, the erection of the first minaret in Delhi as the date before which the President of India was referring.

Ancient Indian democracy is much older than such a timeline. The Manu Smriti (मनुस्मृति), a law code which refers to kingship and the brahmans as important, is rather monarchical, as is the Arthasastra (अर्थशास्त्रम्) of Kauṭilya (चाणक्य). This implies that the Maurya Empire as well as the Gupta Empire do not concern us here. The Pali Canon, the earliest version of the Buddhist scriptures, is written in an Indian language derived from Sanskrit.

If one turns to Sanskrit, Pāṇini (पाणिनि - 6th or 4th century BC) in his Aṣṭādhyāyī (अष्टाध्यायी) offers evidence of such democratic communities. They are known as *janapada* (जानपद). They are mentioned in Panini, and the Rigveda. Some of these communities were ruled by kings, while others seemed to be akin to republics. The Greek historian Arrian seems to refer to such cities as 'free and independent' in his account of Alexander the Great's campaign in India (Arrian Anabasis 5.5). These are identified by the term *saṃgha* (संघ) in Panini. This is controversial for several academics, but not for the president of India who has referred to pre-colonial democracies in India, following in the steps of the research of Kashi Prasad Jayaswal. The controversy is not the term janapada or samghas defined by Panini, but to what they refer. There is endless scholarship on whether ancient Greek democracy was democratic according to today's definitions.

Homeric assemblies promoted discussion and even disagreement (Agamemnon and Achilles). Indeed, there are democratic elements in the assemblies of kings of the *Iliad*. Homer says that it is best to have person to decide rather than a group of leaders (*οὐκ ἀγαθὸν πολυκοιρανίη: εἷς κοίρανος ἔστω*, "*it is not good to have many leaders, let there be one*" Hom. *Iliad*. 2.188). Such an assembly recalls the samiti/sabha of the RigVeda. One may recall the prayer for harmony in the samiti (Rig Veda 10.191.3).

The same debate could be applied to *janapada* or *samghas*. Indian historians have shown that at the time of Panini (after the Rig Veda) these assemblies were democratic and sometimes had no kings. Were *janapadas/samghas* Hindu democracies? Leaving definitions aside, the President of India has today promoted the idea that ancient Indian democracies did exist in the precolonial era.

38

THE POPE'S RUSSIA PROBLEM

3rd September 2023

Pope Francis on the 25th of August 2023 praised Russian imperialism. He named Peter the Great and Catherine II as notable examples of Russian culture.

"You are the descendants of great Russia: the great Russia of saints, rulers, the great Russia of Peter I, Catherine II, that empire – educated, great culture and great humanity."

He did this for a Catholic audience in Russia who was watching his speech at the Meeting of the Catholic Youth of Russia via video link from the church of Saint Catherine's in Saint Petersburg (1783). The church was built by Catherine II for her Polish friend, Stanislas II Augustus Poniatowski, last king of Poland before Russia annexed a large part of it (third partition of Poland in 1795). She brought the treasures of the entire country from Poland to Russia. These were returned after 1921 when Poland defeated the Soviet Union and asked these state treasures to be given back to Poland (among which were the tents of Kara Mustafa from the siege of Vienna in 1683, seized by Jan III Sobieski). The body of Stanislas II Augustus Poniatowski was sent back to Poland before the church of Saint Catherine's was turned into a storeroom by Stalin.

The Pope is now promoting Russian culture and imperialism. This is ironic given that when Pope Clement XIV abolished the Jesuit order in 1773, it was Frederick the Great of Prussia (1740-1786) and Catherine II of Russia (1762-1796) who refused to enact the Catholic law and allowed them to continue within their realms. Jesuits were protected by an Orthodox and a Protestant ruler. Pope Francis is praising Catherine II, who partitioned Poland and refused to enact papal rules concerning the Catholic church within her country. The Russian attitude towards the Jesuit order and Catholic church created the extraordinary image of corruption and bigotry of the Grand Inquisitor written by Dostoyevsky in his novel Brothers Karamazov (1880).

Several Catholics within NATO are astonished by the Pope's preference for Russian Orthodox political power as interpreted in the Kremlin over the Catholic faithful. There are 750,000 Catholics in Russia. There are 4.5-6.5 million Catholics in Ukraine. Poland, which is Catholic by vast majority, is opposed to Russia, especially because of the invasion of Ukraine. Poland has 33 million registered Catholics. The Pope seems unaware of the fundamental anti-Catholic bias of the Russian Orthodox. He does not seem to care. He is not interested in the anti-Russian bias of many Eastern European Catholics. The Pope's statement reveals that he is not pro-Russia, he is anti-NATO. Most of his priestly life (ordained in 1969) was served in the obedience of John Paul II, a Polish Pope who actively worked towards the collapse of the Soviet Union. Pope Francis served and obeyed John Paul II from 1978 to 2005.

It is a new world: the Pope appears more concerned with extra-European questions. The country which unofficially is worried about NATO and losing Russia, as a potential ally, is China. There are 1.4 million Catholics in China. The economic growth of China would mean that they could contribute more significantly to Vatican finances. The anti-NATO position is surprising, given that the alliance is not fighting now. The President of Ukraine on the 13th of December 2022, on the Letterman Show, made a joke about two men who are discussing the war:

"Who is fighting?"
"NATO and Russia"
"How is it going?"

"There is tremendous loss of life, equipment, and the economy is bad for Russia"
"And NATO?"
"NATO hasn't appeared yet".

Technically NATO is at peace. The Pope is against a group of countries which represent over 250 million Catholics. He is in favour of an Orthodox country which has aggressed a neighbouring nation with an Orthodox majority of more than 70 percent of the population. Many Catholics are looking in disbelief.

The Pope's problem is Russia.

39

INDIA BY SEA OR BY LAND? CASTLEREAGH VS NAPOLEON

29ᵗʰ September 2023

India has two main routes of trade with Europe: by sea or by land. The Europeans fought amongst each other to have access to one of these routes. The fight continues today. Napoleon signed a peace treaty with Tzar Alexander I in Tilsit in 1807 to establish a land route from France to India, via the Ottoman Empire and Persia. This was a French answer to the British policy forged and lead by Castlereagh, foreign minister of the United Kingdom. While he was minister for war, the UK defeated Holland. The British, as victors, could decide what to do with the Dutch colonies. Castlereagh thought most of them irrelevant to British interests, except for Cape Colony (Cape Town South Africa). In 1806 he sent his friend and fellow Ulsterman to be first British governor of the newly acquired Cape Colony. The French and Russians understood that the UK had gained an important port on the UK – India trade route. Castlereagh had been president of the board of control of the East India Company from 1802 to 1806 (when Delhi came under British control).

Navigating from India directly to South Africa is rather complex, and for this reason Castlereagh signed the agreement in 1820 by which the United Arab Emirates were recognised as a sovereign state by the UK which offered them protection. When Europeans look at the Napoleonic battles, the superficial interests appear to be on continental Europe, while the important political and commercial aim was favourable conditions for exchanges with India. The same occurred in World War one, when the Germans, allied with Ottoman Turks sought to develop the so-called Istanbul – Mecca railway. The service was part of the more important Berlin to Baghdad line. Once more the aim was a land route from India to Europe. This was the railway line which Lawerence of Arabia famously blew up during his participation in the Arab Revolt against the Ottomans.

Today India wants a sea route. It is called the India-Middle East-Europe corridor. It was announced by prime minister Modi on the 24th of September 2023. The land route is difficult mainly because the north is locked by the highest mountains in the world (called in Sanskrit हिमालय Himalaya, the land of snow). The northwest is, from an

Indian point of view, riddled with diplomatic and military difficulties (as well as religious). President Erdogan of Turkey has reacted by consolidating his position in the Caucasus (Azerbaijan and Nagorno Karabakh, being an example) and with Iraq, and proposed a land route very reminiscent of the Berlin to Baghdad route. However, the sea route could cut off Iraq and Turkey from European and Indian trade.

What Modi and Castlereagh have in common is a capacity to look at a map without prejudice.

The novelty is Greece. While trade between Greek speakers and India is at least 2500 years old, contemporary Greece appears to have what India needs to access the sea efficiently: one of the largest commercial fleets in the world.

India has chosen the sea.

40

SELF-DETERMINATION AND ETHNIC CLEANSING

6ᵗʰ October 2023

Knowledge is trouble. The decline in education is based on the idea that knowing things is troublesome and therefore not knowing means not having trouble. Culture is discussion among different opinions. Often great culture emerges from conflicting local opinions. Even jokes are useful, a manner of diffusing tensions between communities which are regularly in touch but find each other different or even difficult to understand.

The fashionable international solution is to cut conflict and discussion by separating peoples. Woodrow Wilson on the 8ᵗʰ January 1918, proposed self-determination in his 14 points. He later stated: "*National aspirations must be respected; people may now be dominated and governed only by their own consent. 'Self-determination' is not a mere phrase; it is an imperative principle of action*". Each group which felt homogeneous could and should ask to become an independent country. Lenin had already said it in 1914.

This has been a time bomb for Europe and elsewhere. The idea is that if a people within a country is linguistically, culturally, and even ethnically identical there would be no conflict. The idea that having a minority is a problem rather than the source of exchanges which generate culture.

Ireland was one of the first countries to benefit from such self-determination in 1922. The result was that all Irish protestants living in southern Ireland were expelled or emigrated. Moreover, one could point out that the great age of the Celtic revival occurred precisely when some in Ireland felt animosity within the UK, not after it had left it. Eastern Europe became populated with countries which became internally more homogeneous but could not withstand the German and Soviets attacks starting in 1939 leading to World War II. To fight this problem, after the war, the European Union was created, a mix of different traditions and heritages, in opposition to the spirit of self-determination. The displacement of minorities was viewed as the solution for the breakup of Yugoslavia. European countries started recognizing the independence of countries and turned away when it led to trouble for their minorities. Slovenia seemed to be the only country which suffered less from this problem: a small

162

homogeneous country. Croatia, Bosnia, and Serbia received the lion's share of trouble from self-determination. People died or moved. The displacement of peoples is effectively ethnic cleansing. The aim had been to make sure that each geographic area would not have a minority.

In Northern Ireland, the international community is told the west is Catholic and republican and the East is Protestant and unionist. This simplistic notion forgets the infinite local differences and the shared past and present of many mixed communities. Indeed, the principle of self-determination and ethnic cleansing opposes mixed communities, in which people of different traditions live together. Such a mixture promotes cultural creativity. Belfast before 1998 had ten peace walls, cement walls which separate quarters within the city. Since the Good Friday/Belfast agreement in 1998 there are over one hundred of such walls. The principle of peace, as seen from abroad, is to separate and ethnically cleanse areas. Mixed families are the first to suffer from such childish simplicity.

Democracy is about the defence of the minorities interests within the decisions taken by the majority. It is not the removal or elimination of the minority. The alternative is the suppression of minorities as Hitler proposed and executed in the lands, he occupied during World War II.

Today we are petrified looking at Nagorno Karabakh. The inaction of the international community tangled and lost in notions of self-determination and ethnic cleansing is appalling. It appears that an entire population has decided to eradicate its roots and live in a country where some have considered them eccentric and even troublemakers. They cannot go back to their homeland for fear of reprisal. This situation is becoming rather common in Europe and around the world. One may think that Cyprus was a mixed society, which is now segregated and divided.

Passport diplomacy does not help. Ireland, Russia, and other countries offer passports for those who fulfil citizenship criteria, even if born and living abroad. Many Bosnians have either Croatian or Serbian passports even though they were born and have always lived in Bosnia.
Equality before the law means that each should be treated equally in the justice system, not that each person needs to be identical to his or her neighbour.
Diversity in society, but equality before the law, was introduced by the emperor Caracalla in 212 AD when he declared that all people living within the borders of the Roman Empire were Roman citizens.

Borders define citizenship, not ethnic purity derived from self-determination.

41

GAZA AND INDIA

20th October 2023

Modi proposed a Europe Middle East India corridor during the G20 on the 24th of September 2023. The planned route would pass through Saudi Arabia and Israel. From there goods would be shipped to Europe. Which port is India thinking of? While Gaza was part of the Roman empire (63bc-638ad) it was an important port on the Mediterranean Sea. The coastline in that port of the world has few viable deep seaports. Gaza, and its port (Maiuma), was one of them.

The current conflict between Hamas and Israel makes it impossible to imagine Gaza as the preferred port. India may now question reaching the Mediterranean via Saudi Arabia and Israel. It would not be a question of political convenience or even geopolitics. It would be the extra cost of insuring such transportation. No insurance company would guarantee goods in a conflict zone, at a reasonable price. Egypt and the Suez Canal is still a viable option unless a change of regime occurred there, possibly under the influence of parties which look favourably to the Muslim Brotherhood. Qatar and Turkey had been cut off from Modi's trade route and so must be relieved.

However, it brings back old memories of the Roman Empire. In the sixth century, Procopius explained that trade of goods from India to Africa was disrupted by Persians and Arabs.

"For it was impossible for the Ethiopians to buy silk from the Indians, for the Persian merchants always locate themselves at the very harbours where the Indian ships first put in, (since they inhabit the adjoining country), and are accustomed to buy the whole cargoes; and it seemed to the Homeritae a difficult thing to cross a country which was a desert and which extended so far that a long time was required for the journey across it, and then to go against a people much more warlike than themselves." (Procopius De Bellis 1.20.12 Wirth)

If trade routes today were disrupted today by Iran and Gulf States, India would have to transport goods to Africa and then round Cape of Good Hope (South Africa) and reach Europe or even the United Kingdom. This was the preferred British route to India. France, Germany, Russia and the Ottoman empire during the nineteenth century had tried to open a land route to India. (for example, Berlin to Baghdad train line). Turkey and China have proposed being directly connected via the Belt Road Initiative, which would bring goods from China to Europe by land. If India found itself without a land route, it may have to circumnavigate Africa. This however would require a government in South Africa which were more favourable to India's economic outlook.

Given that stability means ease of trade, India is clearly looking to Gaza.

INDEX

171

ABOUT THE AUTHOR

Frederick Lauritzen co-founded Kallipolis.co.uk with Avedis Hadjian in 2022. He read Greats at New College, Oxford (1996-2000, BA, MA) and obtained a doctorate in Classics from Columbia University in New York (2000-2005 MA, MPhil, PhD) with a thesis on Byzantine Literature (published in 2013). From 2008 to 2014 he was a postdoctoral researcher in Bologna and, since 2017, historian at the Scuola Grande di San Marco in Venice.

He is on the advisory board of the Together UK Foundation.

Contact: fredericklauritzen@kallipolis.co.uk

Printed by Amazon Italia Logistica S.r.l.
Torrazza Piemonte (TO), Italy

55965836R00109